Jonathan Norcross

The History of Democracy

Considered as a Party Name and as a Political Organization

.

Jonathan Norcross

The History of Democracy
Considered as a Party Name and as a Political Organization

ISBN/EAN: 9783337078812

Printed in Europe, USA, Canada, Australia, Japan

Cover: Foto ©Suzi / pixelio.de

More available books at **www.hansebooks.com**

THE

HISTORY OF DEMOCRACY

CONSIDERED AS A PARTY NAME AND AS A

POLITICAL ORGANIZATION

BY

JONATHAN NORCROSS

AUTHOR OF "THE CONFLICT OF LABOR AND CAPITAL," "COMMON-SENSE VIEWS OF
STATE SOVEREIGNTY *versus* UNITED STATES SUPREMACY," "DEMOC-
RACY EXAMINED," ETC., ETC.

———

NEW YORK

PUBLISHED FOR THE AUTHOR BY

G. P. PUTNAM'S SONS

1883

CONTENTS.

iv   CONTENTS.

THE HISTORY OF DEMOCRACY CONSIDERED AS A PARTY NAME AND AS A POLITICAL ORGANIZATION.

CHAPTER I.

INTRODUCTORY.

Now that sectional and partisan strifes for sectional and partisan purposes are greatly abated, and those who read can give more attention to the principles and influences which lie at the foundation of, and the vices which endanger, free institutions, it is proposed to give in these chapters a historical sketch of the word Democracy as a party name and organization, together with such reflections and inferences as the narration may suggest.

The word Democracy has a variety of meanings. It means, according to popular usage, a government by the people; the same, or nearly the same, as the word Republicanism. In its last analysis, it means no government at all; or it means a despotism the most cruel, galling, and destructive ever known to mankind; or it means a political party and organization which, when in possession of supreme power, knows no rule, precedent, or law for its guidance, except its own will, or the will of its chiefs. It is, therefore, chiefly its history as a party name and organization that it is proposed to give in these articles. There may be some objections to the word Republicanism as a party name, and some dark stains upon its history. If so, it is the duty of some patriot to point them out. I shall content myself with exposing and commenting upon Democracy as a party name and organization. And I trust it will be by no means difficult to show that the word used as a party name or title has almost invariably proved to be, in practice, as far from the abstract or popular meaning of the word as the east is from the west, or as darkness is from light. If, then, this charge can be established from the history of Democracy, such a party ought not to exist, and cannot exist without endangering free institutions and the representative form of government. But if the charge be not well founded, or if it will apply as well to any other party or party name, then the benefits to arise from its investigation should stimulate patriots to enter upon the work. From such an investigation would likely come a truer estimation and correction of party abuses, and a higher elevation and purification of the means for maintaining free government and equal rights, and consequently greater security and safety for the people. But of all this the reader must judge as we proceed with these historical sketches.

CHAPTER II.

DEMOCRACY IN ANCIENT GREECE.

THE history of Greece, or rather the history of Athens, in its relations and intercourse with other parts of Greece, from the days of Solon till the fall of Athens—about two hundred years,—is as thorough and comprehensive as that of any other country. Its poets, historians, orators, and artists, whose works have come down to the present time, are numerous, and such as have enabled modern students to place the history of the people and their wars and politics in glowing light, affording thorough bases for reflection upon such history. But in a study like this only salient points and leading events can be touched upon, as illustrations for the subject in hand.

The first Democratic party of which we have any account sprang into existence in ancient Athens in the days of Solon, about twenty-five hundred years ago, or 600 years B.C. At that time Athens, or the state of Attica, was or had been in a flourishing condition. Letters had been introduced into Greece, and learning, philosophy, architecture, music, and many other arts had made great progress, especially in Athens. Homer and Hesiod had long since produced their immortal poems. The famous Court of the Areopagus and the Senate of Four Hundred had

been in existence time out of mind. A governor, or
archon, was elected for ten years by the people, and
probably all, except the judges of the Areopagus,
who consisted of ex-archons, were elected by popular vote. The Wise Men of Greece, some of whose
moral and political maxims have come down to this
day, had lived and exercised their influence upon the
people of their country.

Attica was a small state comprising not more than
eight or nine hundred square miles of territory, or a
little less than is contained in the State of Rhode
Island. On that small territory there appear to
have long existed Democratic sentiments and local
sovereignty doctrines, founded upon the interests of
the city of Athens, the interests of the level country
adjacent to Athens, and the interests of the hilly or
mountainous districts. These Democratic and local
sovereignty factions often caused the most serious
disturbances and conflicts in the state, the people
joining themselves first to one leader and then to
another, and thus enabling first one leader and then
another to become tyrant of the state.

The peninsula of Greece is situated about midway
in the Mediterranean Sea, adjacent to the continents
of Europe, Asia, and Africa. Its soil was productive,
its mines and minerals were valuable, its climate was
delightful, as it is at this day; and in the absence of
the mariner's compass, the quadrant, and the science
of astronomy and navigation, as understood and employed at this day, Greece was the most favorably
located for maritime commerce and navigation of
any part of the then known world. Nearly all of

her territory was penetrated by gulfs, bays, rivers, and harbors well adapted to shipping. She had adjacent to her coast numerous islands, and large portions of Europe, Asia, and Africa could be reached upon water without passing out of the sight of land. Under these circumstances and favors of Providence, the Greek people became the greatest agricultural, manufacturing, and commercial people of the world, and Athens the chief manufacturing and commercial city of Greece, as well as the chief emporium of learning, philosophy, and arts of every kind. To such an extent had these arts and employments been carried at the time of which we are speaking, that people flocked to Athens from all parts of the world. In the midst of this tempting prosperity, the Athenian capitalists had enlarged and extended credits beyond all prudent limits, and the people had run into debt and imprudent speculations, as they do under such conditions in modern times. But there came, as there does in modern times, from such causes, a financial panic and a crash. Perhaps free trade and excessive importations from Egypt and Phœnicia helped to bring on the panic, and deepen the financial trouble, as did the free-trade principles and excessive importations into the United States produce the fearful crisis of 1837 in this country. But be this as it may, the merchants and manufacturers of Athens failed, the laboring people were thrown out of employment, and poverty and distress came upon all classes except the capitalists, filling the country with tramps and loafers.

In the midst of this distress there arose mobs,

riots, and an insurrection against the government and the wealthy citizens, which soon resulted in the formation of a Democratic party and an aristocratic party as its counterpart. The Democratic party thus formed, demanded the repudiation of all the debts; and secondly, an equal division of all the property among the citizens. But finding this latter demand attended with many difficulties, and formidable opposition from the property-holders, a compromise was effected between the Democracy and the wealthy citizens. This was to invest Solon, one of the Wise Men of Greece, with dictatorial powers, which position being accepted by Solon, he quieted the tumult by abolishing the debts, freeing the debtors from imprisonment, debasing the coin, and allowing the property to remain as it was, in the hands of its owners. Solon also enacted some other laws of a radical character, for the restraint of the Democracy and for the improvement of the manners and morals of the people generally.

Notwithstanding the poetic and romantic accounts of the poverty of Athens in the time of Solon, it had long been a great commercial and industrial emporium. This is evidenced from the facts already mentioned, and that Athens figured largely in the Trojan War, and had frequently sent out military, trading, and colonizing expeditions, and that Solon himself was a merchant, and had accumulated his wealth by foreign trade.

The elements which composed this early Democratic party, and the facility with which it arrayed itself under captivating and different leaders, and on any side of any principle or question, manifest, as we shall see, a striking resemblance to each and every party formed under the name of Democracy from that day to this; and the fearful tragedies and revolutions, enacted in its name, seem to be the predominating characteristics and outgrowth of the word Democracy as a party name.

CHAPTER III.

IT was during the dictatorship of Solon and the struggle between the Democracy and the wealthy and conservative classes in Athens, there sprang into existence the Democratic General Assembly of Five Thousand, which continued as a great political factor in that state for the next two hundred years or more. At the first establishment of this general assembly its members were evidently chosen by popular elections, like the members of our State Legislatures. The number required to pass upon any measure was five thousand. But its powers at that time embraced the veto and ratifying power only, upon the acts of the Areopagus and the Senate of Four Hundred. The right also of censure of the acts of the executive and administrative officers of the state was exercised by this assembly on some occasions. It had at that time no right to originate measures for the consideration of the Senate or Court of the Areopagus. So large an assembly, from so small a state, must, as every one can see, have been incapable of cool deliberation or wise action upon any measure, except by accident, or through and by the means of a loud-mouthed and talented leader; and, in fact, as experience soon demonstrated, it hardly ever served any other purpose than to become

8

a tool or power in the hands of popular and adroit demagogues, for the promotion of their own ambitious purposes. It served mainly as a tub to the great Democratic whale, for its amusement and gratification; or a chess-board in the hands of wily politicians, to play their games upon. The probability is that the leading men of that day foresaw the purposes for which such an assembly could be used, and helped to augment its size to the utmost limits, for their ulterior purposes, as well as for the neutralization of Democratic influence and power.

As before observed, Solon enacted many excellent laws, but before the people had become accustomed to them, and before Solon's death, Pisistratus, an artful and unscrupulous demagogue, who had become very popular with the people, collected a gang of his reckless followers, seized upon the citadel, the treasury, and the government of the state. This act, as a matter of course, greatly alarmed the conservative citizens, and sent them flying from their country. But the rank and file of the Democratic party stood by him and defended him in this despotic act, and what is also true and worthy of remembrance, is the fact that the General Assembly of Five Thousand, and the rank and file of the Democratic party, not only stood by Pisistratus in this desperate and despotic act, but, as a general rule, supported and defended him and his sons, as Tyrants of Athens, for the next fifty years, and until one of his sons was killed and the other driven out of the country by two high and hot-blooded young men, Aristogiton and Harmodius.

It may be some satisfaction to modern Democrats,

and some credit to Democracy in general, to mention
the fact that Pisistratus proved to be a very clever
and successful ruler, who tried to enforce the laws of
Solon, reinforced by his own despotic power, which
part of the game Solon condemned. And it may be
further mentioned as a comfort to modern Democrats, that the Democratic leaders of Greece, or
especially of Athens, were generally men of military
renown, and men of learning, eloquence, and ability;
and that they, as a rule, when in possession of
supreme and despotic power, gave protection to the
citizens, to the rights of property, and encouragement to all the arts and enterprises which contributed to the grandeur and greatness of the state;
and which probably comprise the only way and
the only methods by which Democracy ever contributed to the fame of the Grecian states,—if, indeed, this fame and name were ever any benefit,
political or moral, to the people of Greece. Nor
is it to be denied, divided as the Greek states were,
one from another, on the Democratic state-sovereignty theory, and governed, as they generally
were, by tyrannical rulers of some kind, they could
not have carried on the military enterprises in which
they were generally engaged, one state or more
against the others, without such despotisms. Nor
without such rule and such a state of affairs in enlightened Greece, could the history of so many intes-
tine and fratricidal wars have been handed down to
succeeding generations and nations for their enlightenment and admonition.

But whether such principles, such governments,

and such results are what is meant by a Democratic party and Democratic rule at this day, form questions worthy the consideration of leading Democrats and other intelligent men. For there are indeed two great facts to be kept in mind in reading the political history of Greece, and especially that of Athens from the days of Solon till the death of Pericles—a space of about two hundred years:—first, the paramount power and influence of the country was in the Democratic party, or rather several Democratic parties in different states; and, secondly, the normal and general condition of the country was internecine war—war among the states and war with foreign nations—rather than a state of peace and quiet; which wars were supported by the agricultural, mineral, and commercial resources of the country, these, as before mentioned, being very great.

It is true, that Pisistratus was twice driven from power, and twice restored, but by what parties or influences we are not fully informed. Yet as the Democratic Assembly of Five Thousand was continued throughout the fifty years' rule of the Pisistratidæ, we are authorized to conclude that their chief support came from the Democratic party.

It may as well be mentioned here as elsewhere, that slavery existed in Athens throughout the entire Democratic era of two hundred years. Nor were the slaves all Africans, but the system included people of all colors and nations, not excepting the native Athenians themselves. And it may also be mentioned, that we have no account of a Democratic party or a Democratic government that ever abolished slavery. It is true we read of several factions and leaders claiming to be Democratic that freed many slaves to make soldiers of them, but as soon as supreme power was obtained by them, as was sometimes the case, the "institution" was restored to its former strength and conditions. If, then, this state of affairs was the normal status, and a part and parcel of the ancient Democracy, as far as our country and times are concerned, this great bone of contention, slavery, having been brushed away in the great Civil War in our country, waged for its maintenance, and our people being a peace and union loving people, rather than a military and fighting people, there would seem to be no further use for a Democratic party in our nation, unless, indeed, it has a mission to uphold, and perpetuate its State-sovereignty theory and inter-State strife, which has been a great part and parcel of Democracy, ever since the days of Solon.[1]

---

[1] The history of ancient Greece, or rather the history of Athens in its relations and intercourse with other parts of Greece, from the days of Solon to the fall of Athens, is probably as full and complete as that of any other nation. The productions of her poets, orators, historians, sculptors, and architects, that have survived the ravages of time, are very numerous, and have enabled modern historians to give us well-digested records. Among the many records given, the "History of Ancient Greece," by George Grote, seems to be the most complete. From its pages many of the facts herein given are derived.

CHAPTER IV.

AFTER the fall of the Pisistratidæ, Athens was
for twenty or more years in great disorder, fluc-
tuating between Democratic and despotic rule, and
between peace and internecine war, when there
arose a popular and talented Democratic leader by
the name of Clisthenes. And although lexicogra-
phers and encyclopedists do not give Clisthenes prom-
inence, some historians claim him as the most astute
politician and leader that Athens had as yet found.
This man observed that the Democrats were becoming tired of being called sovereigns without the enjoyment of the rewards which sovereignty had been
claimed to impart, or what was pretty near the same
thing, the Democrats had acquired an insatiable appetite for the spoils of office, probably such as our
Democrats manifested in the days of Andrew Jackson, and such as both Republicans and Democrats
manifest at the present day. Clisthenes also observed that the Athenian Democrats had become
tired of voting year after year for the learned,
rich, and artful demagogues for fat and influential
places, while they, the voters, were left out in the
cold. This condition of things, it is true, might have
obtained, had the party been called Republican, or

by any other name, as we see political partisans act
under similar circumstances in our country at the
present day. All I claim as peculiar to the Democracy
is that the feat,—the revolution—which then took
place, never could have taken place, in a free country,
under any other name or party organization ever
known to mankind, for the reason that no other
party ever formed contained the elements to be so
readily induced to turn upon and trample under foot
and into the dust its own professed principles, or a
principle so essential to the liberties of mankind as
the elective franchise.

Clisthenes having gained the confidence of the
Democrats, and full control of the party, proposed
to divide and did divide, the people of Attica into
ten tribes or sections, called by some historians
" cantons." Up to this time the people had been
divided into four tribes or classes, according to their
wealth and standing, for political purposes. Each of
Clisthenes' ten tribes was to contain as near as practicable an equal number of citizens, without distinction of rank, standing, or wealth. He then took
from each of these tribes, by lot or draft, six hundred
men, making in all six thousand. He then provided
for drawing five hundred men from each six hundred, to serve as legislators in the General Assembly
of Five Thousand. The surplus—one hundred—from
each tribe to stand as supernumeraries, from which
the general assembly could be kept full up to five
thousand, which was the legal quorum for the transaction of business. Nor did the lot or draft stop
with the general assembly. All the civil offices of

the state, including archons, were filled by lot or draft in a similar way, except perhaps a very few places, where great learning and efficiency were absolutely necessary to keep the state from falling into complete paralysis or anarchy, and these were appointed by the general assembly. And what is also worthy of note is the fact that the generals and other high officers of the army were appointed by the General Assembly of Five Thousand. I say by the general assembly, for the truth is, from that day forth, as history shows, the government of Athens became a military despotism, under the name of Democracy; the general assembly and all the civil offices becoming mainly places for recording the acts and wishes of the successful generals of the army, and for the performance of police duties, in accordance with the commanding general's orders.

Or perhaps it should be further observed that the General Assembly of Five Thousand became a forum of debate, and was used mainly for generals and orators in their conflicts one with another; the executive power being always lodged in the hands of the most successful general or orator, the civil authority being as completely swallowed up in the military as it is in the island of Cuba under the rule of Spain. And thus were the elective franchise and popular elections abolished, at one fell swoop, by the Democratic party.

Does any one ask what reason can be given for this revolution? I will venture two or three. First, it was intended to gratify the morbid appetite of the Democracy for the spoils of office, without regard to capacity or merit. Second, to cripple the efforts of the learned, the wealthy, and intelligent portion of society, which ordinarily got into office under the elective franchise. And thirdly, as a means, in the hands of the ambitious, of upholding military and despotic power by the force of Democratic numbers, and their partiality for despotism.

It is possible that this system of government, which continued in Athens for near two hundred years, and to some extent in other Greek states, was as well adapted to the rambling adventurers and warlike spirits of the Greeks, and especially to the inhabitants of Athens at that time, as any other system that could have been devised by man. But be this as it may, it eventually operated to bring the city of Athens, after a series of wars upon wars, to a condition when "all the Athenians and strangers which were there spent their time in nothing else but either to tell or to hear some new thing." This state of affairs, however, as expressed by St. Paul, came to pass several centuries after the days of Clisthenes ; hence it is our duty to speak more particularly of the immediate and near results of this Clisthenic revolution, which, as before observed, not only abolished popular elections, both for the general assembly and other places of honor and trust, but actually operated in the near future to abolish the Senate of Four Hundred, by causing its members to be appointed by this general assembly. It also caused the Court of the Areopagus to disappear, or become a mockery of its former self, by virtue of the archons, from whom it had been made up, being

selected by lot from the mass of the citizens, probably under the same spirit in which it was proposed
to abolish the Senate and the Supreme Court of the
United States, under the administration of Andrew
Jackson.   In truth, this Democratic General Assembly of Five Thousand soon absorbed or abolished
all other legislative and judicial departments of the
government, and invested, or pretended to invest,
their powers in this great assembly. All of which results, as a matter of course, were brought about by
the dictation of ambitious Democratic leaders and
supporters of this Clisthenic constitution, who
chose to have all real obstacles to their despotic influence and power removed from their path.

It may be said, and probably with some truth,
that through and by means of this Clisthenic constitution, the learned, the wealthy, and the intelligent
citizens came into influence and power as military
men, with less trouble than through and by means
of the elective franchise in the hands of the citizens,
and got rid of the noise, expense, and uncertainty of
popular elections. And it is also probable that the
lot system was favored by the common people, or at
least by extreme and bigoted Democrats, because
they came into small places of honor and trust
with far less trouble and uncertainty. The size of
the general assembly in so small a state as Attica,
and other numerous small offices, rendered it almost
certain that each voter could come into some office
or place of honor as often as once in four or five
years; which was counted much better than to be
always out in the cold, and destitute of all official
influence throughout their lives.

Or it may be possible that the popular elections, under Democratic rule and manipulations for many years, had become slightly corrupt. It may be that ballot-box stuffings, false counting and returning of votes, and tissue ballots, had become common. Or it may be that false naturalization papers and colonization of voters were employed; and possibly corner and cross-road groceries were numerous, and stocked with mean whisky or other drinks to influence voters, and that drunkenness had become the order of the day, especially on election days. Or perhaps it had become the practice of Democratic voters to support the most unscrupulous rascals for office, rather than the most honest and capable men: and hence those grand old immaculate Democratic leaders, such as Pisistratus, Clisthenes, and Pericles, instead of enacting efficient electoral laws, came to the conclusion that the best way to purify the ballot-box was to abolish it altogether, substituting the draft in its place, with a plenty of small offices for the entertainment and occupancy of the sovereigns; they, the great leaders, taking the state and its entire affairs into their own hands, for the special benefit of the sovereigns, and as a matter of patriotic devotion to their beloved country.

Some old Whigs of much experience in political affairs insinuate that our Democratic brethren of to-day have only transferred these arts, tricks, and vices at elections from their Greek prototypes, and that, like them, they are very fond of change, of something new, of something startling and revolutionary, even, if need be, to the substitution of the lottery-

box for the ballot-box, and that we should, therefore, be as charitable as possible to the idiosyncrasies
of the ancient and modern Democracy, and try to
hold them to the practices and principles of our
Republican fathers.

Query: - Has a Democratic party ever been known
to improve or reform election laws?

CHAPTER V.

No doubt many readers are astonished at the account given in the last chapter about the Athenian Democracy, and the exchange they made of the ballot-box for the lottery-box, in the selection of civil officials, both high and low. Yet it is substantially true, if the most learned and minute historians are to be believed.

Under the Clisthenic constitution more changes were wrought in the machinery and polity of the government of Attica than can here be described. At first, instead of one general of the army, there were ten, one for each tribe ; which Democratic law, as a matter of course, when war came, produced anarchy, unless all gave way to one commander-in-chief, as in the battle of Marathon. The courts were a kind of committees of safety, or lynching parties. Under one of these courts, Socrates, the great philosopher of his age, whose virtues and sayings gave great celebrity to Greek philosophy, was tried, convicted, and executed, and in a short time thereafter, another Democratic court of the same kind tried, convicted, and executed his judges, for putting to death so great and good a man.

Under this constitution the law of ostracism was

20

instituted, by which any political leader or aspirant who became obnoxious to the Democracy, or who was troublesome in the Assembly of Five Thousand could be banished from the state by six thousand votes cast for the purpose. Under it Themistocles, Aristides, Cimon, and other great men of Athens, distinguished for their services, were driven from their homes and their country into exile. This law was somewhat in advance of the barbaric methods of driving out with arms, or assassinating obnoxious leaders, that had before been practised in Greece and the surrounding nations, and somewhat in advance of old-fashioned Democratic local-sovereignty practices of disposing of obnoxious chiefs, among the American Indian tribes, by slaughter. Of course, we do not here insinuate that the Democracy of to-day wish to revive the law of ostracism, but allude to it because it was a method of disposing of troublesome opponents without a trial before court and jury, or without the long and tedious political campaigns which are required for the overthrow in our country of such men as John Quincy Adams, Henry Clay, John C. Calhoun, and John McPherson Berrien, and other obstinate and troublesome old Whigs. Nevertheless, the ostracism was a purely Democratic institution, and the best method at that time known to the Democracy of getting rid of obnoxious leaders.

It would be impracticable, in briefly tracing the history of Athenian Democracy, to name all the riots, tumults, enterprises, and wars with which the old Democratic leaders regaled themselves and the people. The truth is, the General Assembly of Five Thousand was very much like the modern mass-meeting, before which the orators could air themselves, while there was no legal right or power to get up a counter mass-meeting. It therefore virtually placed all great questions, civil and military, of peace and of war, in the hands of their great chieftains, generals, and orators, and who, by virtue of control once gained, wielded the entire power of the state, making war, or making peace, as best suited their views and interests, the vast assembly being well adapted to promote such despotism; if indeed it can be called-despotism where a great leader has corrupted the people, and has a great assembly of the people at his back to second his designs, and register and enforce the sentiments and decrees he may advance, and busy itself with appointing and removing members of the police, and other small matters.

From the time when the great Democratic Assembly of Five Thousand was instituted, and more especially from the time when, for the selection of officials, the lottery-box was substituted for the ballot-box, down to the days of Pericles, the Democracy of Athens seems never to have doubted that the party possessed and enjoyed the sovereign power of the state, and that all had been done that could be done to strengthen and perpetuate the rights and liberties of the citizens, albeit a large portion of the people were all the while in slavery, and all the great leaders were taken from the old aristocratic families who had no use for the common people except as soldiers to fight their battles, and when, if ever, they

failed to come up to their call, they generally liberated, and made enough soldiers from the slaves to
bring them to terms, thus enlarging the Democratic
idea and area of liberty.

CHAPTER VI.

BUT, as before hinted, whether the influence and power of these great leaders were acquired by their swords in domestic broils, in foreign wars, or by the force of their oratory, the position of leadership once established, their next ambition was to contribute to the wealth, grandeur, and greatness of Athens. This was their chief political economy, if any they had, and in this the entire population, Democratic and aristocratic, co-operated with the utmost enthusiasm. And hence it came to pass, notwithstanding the frequent domestic broils growing out of the competition of aspirants for supremacy, that Athens, from the encouragement of the industrial and liberal arts, schools, commerce, and shipping, and from successful wars and alliances with other states and provinces, became by far the most beautiful and wealthy city on the Mediterranean, and attracted more visitors than any other city in the known world. Athens had, at the time of which we are speaking, one thousand tributary cities and provinces. Her treasury was overflowing with money. Her people revelled in luxury and extravagance, and rolled the despotic sway of their leaders as a sweet morsel under their tongues. Words would fail to paint the Sybaritic folly and pride to which Democratic institutions had carried the people.

A learned writer of Greek history, in speaking of the morals and manners of Athens at that time, says: "Instead of the bread, herbs, and simple fare recommended by the laws of Solon, the Athenians availed themselves of their extensive commerce to import the delicacies of distant countries. The wines of Cyprus were cooled with snow in summer; in winter the most delightful flowers adorned the tables and persons of wealthy Athenians. Nor was it sufficient to be crowned with roses, unless they were likewise annointed with the most precious perfumes. Parasites, dancers, and buffoons were a usual appendage of every entertainment. Among the weaker sex, the passion for delicate birds, distinguished for their voice and plumage, was carried to such excess as to merit the name of madness." And in speaking of the political condition of the people, he says: "The Grecian history of those times affords a more striking contrast than ever appeared in any other age or country of wisdom and folly, of magnanimity and meanness, of liberty and tyranny, of simplicity and refinement, of austerity and voluptuousness." This is a striking description, but by no means an incorrect one, of the moral and political condition unavoidably springing from Democracy as a party name and organization in possession of the supreme power of the state.

Under these circumstances, about one hundred years after the days of Solon, and forty years after the Persian invasion and its overthrow, Pericles, the most talented and ambitious man of his age, came upon the stage as a Democratic leader.

Pericles was born, grew to manhood, and came to notoriety and influence under the Clisthenic constitution. He had several competitors for popularity. But being a general in the army, a sagacious politician, and accomplished orator, he rose rapidly, and soon became sole dictator of Attica, and her affiliated states, cities, and provinces; and what may seem almost incredible to those who have not studied the history of the Greek Democracy, is the fact that he ruled and directed the affairs of Attica and her allies as with a rod of iron, for forty consecutive years, without ever having received a civil appointment, unless it was in the form of a request to deliver an oration to the people. All his influence and power, and especially over the Democratic Assembly of Five Thousand, came from his generalship in the army and his great power as an orator. By means of these and a few unscrupulous political bummers, he swayed and controlled the Democracy, and through them the state, as effectually as a pedagogue controls a crowd of noisy urchins, or as a herdsman his bleating flocks.

But he had not long attained to this perilous height of power, before he commenced plundering the allies, and using the funds which they had contributed to the public treasury, for general purposes, for the adornment and enriching of Athens; and so many grand edifices, monuments, temples, theatres, arches, statues, and fortifications did he put

on foot, and push so rapidly to completion, that almost before the allies were aware of it, the public
funds and common treasury and revenues were
all absorbed. But as soon as these facts became
known, the allies began to revolt. Nor was it long
before Sparta and her allies were co-operating with
these revolting allies, and making war upon Attica.
This was called the Second Peloponnesian War, and
lasted twenty-seven years. In the midst of it the
plague broke out in Athens, and raged with great
violence, probably for the want of suitable food,
clothing, and shelter, as Athens was then besieged
by Sparta and her allies. Pericles himself took the
contagion, and became one of its victims, and died
in the strength of his manhood, amid the terrible
throes of his country, which he had himself caused.
But the war went on, and only ended in the fall and
sack of that large and beautiful city, and the setting
up in her midst of the Thirty Tyrants, a catastrophe
hardly more complimentary to the Greek Democracy than the fall of Jerusalem under Titus to the
Jewish hierarchy.

It is not to be forgotten, or denied, that each
supreme government, like each head of a family,
often finds itself in a condition to so concentrate its
powers and discount its resources as to live in luxury
and extravagance for a short time, and thus so captivating and corrupting its constituents as to soon
plunge them into idleness, imbecility, poverty, and
ruin. The resources of Athens, at the time of which
we are speaking, as before stated, were almost bound-
less. Her commanding position, her shipping, and

her enterprising merchants had, like London at the present time, made nearly the whole world tributary to her wealth. As it was said of Jerusalem in the days of Solomon, four or five hundred years earlier, " silver and gold was as plenteous in her streets as stones," and her Democratic despots, being destitute or regardless of God and the true principles of morality and political economy, and having great power and influence over the people, by fraud and military force, caused the wealth of other parts of the world to be appropriated to the gratification of Athenian appetites, vanity, and pride; first, by theatrical entertainments, then by splendid architecture, statuary, and fortifications round about the city. But against all such pride, folly, and wickedness, mankind soon revolted, and in the providence of God, the doomed city was brought to retribution, thus affording a great moral and political lesson to succeeding generations. Our own country has already experienced a bitter dose of this despotic, alias Democratic, perverseness, and wise, happy, and fortunate will our people be, if in the future they avoid the vanity and pride which inevitably lead to the destruction and ruin of the generations yielding to them.

It is not the design of these articles to discourse learnedly on Greek history, arts, and civilization, except so far as to trace the Democratic features of the Greek governments, and especially of the government of Athens, and the effect these features had upon the Greek people until the fall of Athens, as indicated in our last chapter. This I have endeavored to do, both in letter and spirit, in accordance with the most authentic history. If, in faithfully doing this, it exhibits Democracy as a name and party organization in possession of supreme political power, the most exclusive and tyrannical, the most hypocritical and corrupting system that ever afflicted and ruined any enlightened community, that is to be ascribed to the system itself, to its inherent depravity rather than to the natural depravity of mankind; and if it should be made manifest before we get through that Democracy as a party name and organization is always the same depraved and corrupting system, it is to be ascribed to the same inherent cause, and the labor that is required to present these facts should be counted a duty which devolves upon every student of sound and safe government and well-regulated liberty. And if our Democratic brethren of the present day can make out better qualities, or give us a better history of a Democratic party, the people of this country will doubtless be glad to consider such views. Sound and safe government and well-regulated liberty spring from and rest upon wisdom, virtue, justice, and peace, and not upon vice, cruelty, and war, such as seemed to be the animating forces among the Greeks under Democratic rule.

Now, Democracy as a sentiment is a very good thing where the people are scarce, as they were in the early American settlements, and all are intelligent, moral, honest, and law-abiding, and where the homesteads are twenty miles apart, and where, if every man does as he pleases, he will not trespass upon his neighbors' rights. But where people are numerous and compact, and where the relations and dependencies of life are almost infinite in number, the "everybody do as you please" sentiment is nothing but hypocritical cant, that soon contradicts itself by rallying around the greatest demagogue in the land as a leader, and by howling for the most proscriptive and oppressive measures that cruelty can invent, such as were often practised among the Greeks in the name of Democracy. It is true, concentrated political power in a numerous community is a good and necessary thing, but when we form or find a political party which knows and will tolerate no other method than that of a despotic chief in whom to invest this necessary power, and a party which counts its will, and his will, above all law, as was done under the old Greek Democracy, Democracy becomes a sentiment and system utterly destructive of sound and safe government, and drives the most learned, virtuous, and patriotic citizens into practices and manners which are destructive of civilization itself, as abundantly indicated in the history of Democracy in Greece, and in the fall of Athens, " the head and centre" of its spirit and influence.

The most noted and brilliant days of Athens were those including and following the battles of Thermopylæ, Platea, and Salamis, by which the Persians were driven from Greek territory, to the fall of Athens,—a space of about seventy years,—forty years of which Pericles was absolute ruler. These were also the most pompous days of Democracy. From the days of Solon to the close of this Persian War Democracy and oligarchy were constantly struggling for

supremacy, and hence it is hard to say whether
Democracy or oligarchy is entitled to the most
credit in those splendid victories over the Persians,
or whether the native energy, genius, and bravery
of the Greeks gained those great achievements in
spite of both. Wherever the merit lay, one thing is
certain, they (the victories) placed the state of Attica
and the Greeks as a nation in the most commanding
position for good or for evil of which we have any
account in ancient history, unless we except the
Israelites in the days of David and Solomon. And
had the people possessed the virtue and patriotism
sufficient to have formed and maintained a firm
national government, according to human reasoning
they must have long continued the most powerful
people in the world. But Democracy and its most
intimate relative and companion, state sovereignty,
having full sway, soon culminated in a catastrophe
that wrecked the most enlightened people known,
and shook the then civilized world from centre to
circumference. It might almost be said in the language of Milton :

> " Earth felt the wound, and Nature from her seat,
> Sighing through all her works, gave signs of woe
> That all was lost."

We have already quoted from a writer of Greek
history, an account of the morals and manners of the
Athenians which grew up under the Democratic
régime, and we now give the lament of Thucydides
over the twenty-seven years' war, brought on and
continued, as the fruit of Democracy and state
sovereignty combined. He says: "As it exceeded

the ordinary duration of human power or resent-
ment, it was accompanied with unusual circumstances of terror, which to the pious credulity of an
unfortunate age, naturally announced the wrath of
Heaven, justly provoked by human cruelty. Whilst
pestilence and famine multiplied the actual suffer-
ings, eclipses and earthquakes increased the consternation and horror of that lamentable period. Several
warlike communities were expelled from their
hereditary possessions ; others were not only driven
from Greece, but utterly extirpated from the earth ;
some fell a prey to party rage, others to the vengeance of foreign enemies ; some were slowly exhausted by the contagion of a malignant atmosphere ;
others overwhelmed at once by sudden violence ;
while the combined weight of calamity assailed the
power of Athens, and precipitated the downfall of
that republic from the pride of prosperous dominion
to the dejection of dependence and misery."

This short account seems almost incredible, yet it
is unquestionably and literally true, and the fruit and
outgrowth of Democracy in power.

It should be observed, and perhaps should have
been sooner stated, that before the commencement
of this twenty-seven years' war, Athens and Sparta,
the two leading states of Greece, had managed to
absorb all or nearly all the separate Greek communities in Greece proper, in Italy, Ionia, and other
parts of Europe, Asia, and Africa bordering on the
Mediterranean, as allies and dependencies ; and as
each of them gained influence and control over these
separate communities, they tried to force, and did in

the main force, their respective political tenets and forms of government upon them, which, on the part of the Athenians, consisted in their radical Democracy, their large General Assembly, and the despotic leaders which these produced, thus causing the State to be arrogant, dictatorial and quarrelsome ; while on the part of the Spartans, their government was, in the main, hereditary and aristocratic. The main polity of the Spartans had been, under Lycurgus, to make soldiers of all the men, for home defence, and the holding of their slaves in subjection. And the probability is that they never aimed at foreign conquest until they were spurred into such ambitious projects by the restless, aggressive, and quarrelsome disposition of the Athenian Democracy. And hence the just conclusion, both from this disposition and the beginning and events of the Peloponnesian war, is that Democracy was at the bottom of the whole affair, and responsible for the shocking disasters brought upon the civilized world, as described by Thucydides.

From the historical facts now given, it is difficult to see how our Democratic brethren of to-day can draw any consolation, encouragement, or comfort from their brethren, or prototypes, in old Greece, or how they can fail to draw some valuable lessons from their conduct and its consequences. It would seem that instead of holding up, as they do, the Democracy of Greece as a pattern of political philosophy and patriotism, they ought to acknowledge, that the almost incessant wars and frequent domestic tumults in the states where a Democratic party predomi-

nated, are proofs that such a party is a fearful
scourge to any people, and that it is constantly forcing upon them the question, not what style or form
of government is best, but whether the people shall
have a government or no government, or, what is
nearly the same thing, no government, or despotism,
upheld by constant tumults and wars.

And, secondly, it is difficult to see how our
Democratic brethren of to-day can refuse to
acknowledge that under no other system than that
of Democracy and state sovereignty, its intimate relation and constant companion, in so small a country
as that of Greece, and among so enlightened a
people, could so many wars have been engendered,
and one so long and destructive as this twenty-
seven years' war have been kept up. Verily, ye
modern Democrats, you must confess that such
sentiments, such a system, such vices, such crimes,
such ruin as a Democratic party brought upon
Greece, and brings upon every country where it
has full sway, are of such a moral and political
character that Heaven itself is shocked at the spectacle, and wills the destruction and the punishment
of any people who tolerate it.

In speaking of Pericles, the great Athenian
Democratic leader, the same historian from whom
we have quoted, says of him and his administration:

"According to the popular principles which he
professed, he deemed it the duty of a statesman to
provide not merely for the army, the navy, the
judges, and others immediately employed in the

public service; the great body of the people he regarded as the constant and most important object of his ministerial care. The immense revenues of the state, which had hitherto been chiefly squandered in shows and festivals, in gaudy ostentation and perishing luxury, he directed to objects more solid and durable which while they embellished the city, might exercise the industry and display the talents of the citizens. Guided by such motives he boldly opened the treasury, and expended four thousand talents; a sum which then might command as much labor as six or seven millions sterling in the present age. By this liberal encouragement, he animated every art, excited every hand, enlivened every exertion, and called forth into the public service the whole dexterity, skill, and genius of his countrymen; while the motives of gain or glory which he proposed, allured from all quarters the ingenious strangers who readily transported their talents to Athens, as the best market and most conspicuous theatre."

This scrap of history is introduced to our Democratic brethren of to-day to show how lavish a Democratic chieftain can be with public funds, and not be brought to account, when he has a radical Democratic party at his back. And, secondly, to show what a fine time their old Democratic prototypes had with free theatres, free festivals, and free games of every kind. And, thirdly, to show that any political party, in the possession of supreme power, which yields to the passions and follies of the multitude, or cuts loose from precedents, and the time-honored lessons of the ages, is liable, not only to plunge its country into despair, but to be compelled to tear down with its own hands the bulwarks and monuments which its pride and ambition has reared, as the Athenians were obliged to do, under the rule of the Thirty Tyrants placed over them by Lysander, their Spartan conqueror. Such was the terrible fate of the great and proud city of Athens, and thus too was sung the funeral dirge of genuine Democracy throughout all Greece.

We trust that all good Republicans have long since drawn valuable lessons from these historical records, and that both Democratic and all other political parties will profit by them in the future.

The ancient Greeks are counted the most intelligent and highly civilized people in olden times. As stated in a former chapter, the peninsula and country of the Greeks proper did not contain as much territory as the State of South Carolina. But its soil and mines were highly productive, and the best situated for trade and navigation of any part of the world. Reasoning then from natural causes, and the general conduct of mankind in a civilized state, had not the Greeks been overtaken and possessed by the Democratic mania, they must have soon become as great in political economy and statesmanship as they were in literature, arts, and warlike enterprises, as well as the most wealthy nation upon the face of the earth. Every facility, both of land and water, was at their command. Reasoning, therefore, from the size of their country and other causes, it would seem that so intelligent a people could not have been induced by the arts of ambitious men to adopt a form of government, either too weak or too strong, or one which would lead to the depression of their energies, loss of their just liberties, or the destruction of the country. Had they possessed the wisdom and patriotism to form and maintain a firm national government, the world would not have been compelled, while admiring their arts, to behold also the tumults and wars, and their rivers of blood that deluged the country from the days of Pisistratus to the fall of Athens. No man can account for these terrible scenes among so gifted a people, upon any other hypothesis than that they were due to the introduction of the Democratic theory, as developed under such a party name and organization.

We must admit that in that age of the world a purely republican form of government and constitution like that of the United States could not have been conceived, wrought out, and adopted. Even Plato, two hundred years after Pisistratus, could not or did not suggest such a system in his essay on government. But it is not unreasonable to suppose that the Greeks could have adopted and should have adopted some such a system as that of Rome. For it was in the days of Solon that the Romans came to Athens to learn laws and of a government suitable to their own country, which affords evidence that such a system as that of the Romans had been contemplated, or had been in existence in Greece. Had some such system been adopted as that of the Romans, or that of some other nation known to them, it would have doubtless kept them from destroying

each other as they did under the reign of Democracy. Had they adopted some such system of laws
and government as that of the Hebrews under the
Judges, which continued over four hundred years,
their utter ruin under the Democracy might have
been averted.

Nor is this the only view to be taken of the short-
sightedness and culpable course of the Greeks, and
the miserable end to which they were led by the
fascination of the Democratic system.

It is claimed, and not disputed by historians, that
the alphabet and its concomitant arts were introduced into Greece several centuries before Solon.
It is also well known that the Olympic, Isthmian, and
other games and expositions were established about
the same time, the chief object of which was to
"form a bond of union for the Grecian states."
Besides these expositions good and patriotic men
instituted the Amphictyonic Council, made up of
deputies from the various states for the discussion of
religious and political subjects, both of which were
well calculated to produce harmony, and lead to a
national government, and probably would have done
this had not the theory of Democracy and local
sovereignty been sprung upon the people in the time
of Solon. And again there is another point to be
noticed. Some historians claim that the original
governments of the Greek communities were republican in form, like that of the Romans, and that
royalty and tyranny were the exceptions to the general rule, and that for centuries they lived in peace
and harmony; which must be true, as we do not

read of frequent or any great wars between the states before the days of Solon and the rise of Democracy. The conjectures, for we can call them nothing but historical conjectures, that the Greek communities in so small a country, in early times, held little or no intercourse, one with another, would be to place them, in point of civilization, below the North American Indian tribes. They were doubtless for many centuries quiet, peace-loving, and enterprising communities; their religion, such as it was, having a moral and softening influence upon the manners of the people. The only conclusion, therefore, that we can cordially, affectionately, and honestly commend to our Democratic brethren of to-day, is that the introduction of the Democratic and local-sovereignty theory into Greece became the great red dragon that trampled down and stamped out all Grecian civilization and liberty, and reduced the state of Attica from greatness and grandeur to the lowest depths of misery and degradation.

Another learned writer of Greek history in speaking of the Democratic period of the country, says: " We seek in vain, either in the history of Athens or Lacedæmon, for the beautiful idea of a well-ordered commonwealth. The revolutions of government which they were ever experiencing, the external factions with which they were embroiled, plainly demonstrate that there was a radical defect in the structure of the machine, which precluded the possibility of regular motion. The condition of the people under those governments was such as partook more of servitude and oppression, than that of the subjects

of the most despotic monarchies. The slaves formed
the actual majority of the inhabitants in all the
states of Greece. To these the free citizens were
rigorous bond-masters. Bondage being a consequence of the contraction of debts, even by freemen, a great proportion of these was subject to the
tyrannical control of their fellow-citizens. Nor were
the richer classes in the actual enjoyment of independence. They were perpetually divided into factions, which servilely ranked themselves under the
banners of the contending chiefs of the republic.
Those parties were kept together solely by corruption. The whole was therefore a system of servility
and debasement of spirit, which left nothing of a
free or ingenuous nature in the condition of individuals, nor any thing that could furnish encomium
to a real advocate for the dignity of human nature."

It might seem to some that no further comments
were here required on the fearful vices of a Democratic party. But as we have a Democratic party of
our own to deal with, whose sins roll mountain-high
when it is in possession of supreme power, we
must defer such remarks until we come to its own
record. "Sufficient unto the day is the evil thereof."

Modern Democrats, and many other admirers of
Greek literature and arts, point to them as the fruits
of Democratic institutions. This is evidently faulty
reasoning and leads to wrong conclusions, unless it
can be shown that Republicanism and Democracy
are in all respects the same, and that Greece had no

literature and arts before Democracy became pre-
dominant in Greece, and this, as we have shown, it
is not possible to do. The Greeks were a literary
and artistic people centuries before Democracy, as a
party name and organization, was known. Before
the times of Homer and Hesiod, the great poets,
we have accounts of Greek writers whose works
have been lost. This fact is mentioned because
some writers claim that poetry in Greece was
prior to prose writing. To admit this would be
like supposing that architects were prior to car-
penters, that sculptors were prior to masons, or
that historians were prior to school-masters, and
poems prior to primers, all of which must, of
course, be faulty reasoning and wild fancy. Prose
writing must, as a natural consequence, have existed long before poetry was committed to paper or
parchment, and have been contemporary, or nearly
contemporary, with the introduction of the alphabet.
And although poetry may have played an early part
with prose writings, it could not have had currency
and popularity as literature without the simplest and
most practical forms of composition. It must have
been the use of prose writings rather than poetry,
and oratory rather than verse, that enabled the poor
and laboring portions of society to form political
opinions.

And here I venture the opinion for what it may be
worth, that the vast catalogue of Greek gods, demi-
gods, heroes, and heroines was the outgrowth of
prose romances by gifted writers, after the style of
our modern novel-writers, or rather our modern nov-

clists seem to have derived their spirit and life from Grecian mythology. It is impossible to account for the host of characters honored and worshipped by them on any other ground than that there was a class of romance writers and impostors who gave to the gods and heroes character and fascination among the people. The author of almost every sentiment, art, and opinion was deified by these writers. And it is not to be denied that the demoralizing effect of so many lying and licentious gods and goddesses, heroes and heroines, naturally resulted in the development of radical Democracy, with its endless "isms" and impracticable theories. Nor is it by any means discreditable to Christianity and modern civilization, that Democracy is traceable in its origin to the abominable Greek mythology.

It is true that literature and arts blazed forth with great splendor during the reign of Democracy in Greece, or rather in Athens; or especially oratory, architecture, statuary, and licentious poetry, which last requires for its translation in modern times a man whose ethical standard is low. Athenian Democracy established and upheld the General Assembly of Five Thousand, before which great orators aired themselves to great advantage. It also established and upheld the lottery system upon the ruins of the elective franchise, by which these same Democratic orators became the controlling power of the state, and enabled the Athenians to enforce their full-fledged Democratic system in other states. And by this same means all rival assemblies were prevented from acting as a check on this legal assembly, the party, and its leaders thus

virtually overthrowing the popular views of Democratic rights and privileges as understood at this day.
Under these circumstances, it seems quite probable
that political oratory operated as a scourge rather
than a blessing to the people, however much that art
was elevated by such a condition of affairs, and however much it has been imitated in modern times.
And however much also the greatness and grandeur
of Greek architecture and statuary grew up under
Democratic reign, we must bear in mind that nearly
all this greatness and grandeur were built up from
funds plundered from other states and provinces.
Outside of Athens, and aside from the reign of Pericles, the great Democratic leader, we find or read of
no more architecture, statuary, or oratory than is
found in other civilized countries.   And what is also
here worthy of note is the fact, that these great and
grand specimens of architecture and statuary, and
the plunder of funds to construct them, more perhaps
than all other causes, provoked the destruction of
Athens by the other Greek states.

Let us now suppose we have a President of the
United States elected by our present Democratic
party with all the madness and insanity that charac-
terize such a party when in power, and that this
President should take the bits of government into his
teeth, as did Pericles, and that he should be as bold,
talented, and audacious as Pericles was, and should
take it into his head to open the treasury of the
United States, as Andrew Jackson did in 1833, and
remove the public deposits to some other places
selected by himself. But instead of stopping at this

removal, with the two hundred million dollars in
the treasury of the United States as at the present
time, he should say: " I will use forty, thirty, or
even twenty million dollars a year to establish theatres, temples, museums, cathedrals, monuments,
and statuary for the ornamentation and grandeur of
the capital," and that he should be allowed to do all
this, as he certainly would be, under an all-powerful
Democratic party, precisely as Pericles was allowed
to do, and precisely as Jackson was allowed to
to do with the treasury of the United States, in the
removal of the public deposits. Nor is this all imagination and speculation. For when Jackson, the
great Democratic chief of this country, removed in an
illegal and despotic manner the public deposits from
the place of lawful custody to places of his own selection (where they were lost), the Democratic party,
which put him in power, did not offer a single remon-
strance, or utter a word of complaint at the act,
but shouted Bravo! bravo! precisely the same as
the Athenians did at the despotic acts of Pericles.
And when the Senate of the United States ventured
to censure Jackson for this act of despotism, this
same Democratic party beat down and beat out the
old Whigs who opposed this bold proceeding, as
though they were public robbers, and as though
Jackson and his advisers were saints and heroes.
And when Jackson and his followers squandered and
stole the public funds, as they did by the million,
and by the ten million, until the amount swelled to
thirty or forty million dollars, in the course of three
or four years, in the face and eyes of all this, the

Democratic party shouted : " Old Hickory forever !"
and " Great is the Democracy and General Jackson !"
If, we say, a Democratic President with a powerful
Democratic party at his back, which had put him in
power, should attempt such a scheme as that of Pericles, with the two hundred million dollars in our
treasury, and with no more boldness and audacity
than our Democratic leaders have often manifested,
would not all the architects and sculptors, artists and
artisans, and, as for that, all the rascals in the world,
flock to Washington as they flocked to Athens ? and
how long would it be before our modern Athens
would stand forth as the greatest and grandest city
in the world for arts, artists, luxury, and vice of
every kind ?   This is virtually what the Democracy
in its halcyon days did in old Athens, at the expense
and offence of all other parts of Greece, and laid the
foundation for the near-by humiliation and ruin of
Athens itself.   And this is precisely what some great
Democratic leader in the Presidential chair may and
probably will do in this country, when, if ever again,
the party gets full control of our government.

This was the Democratic scheme that made
Athens great and grand in statuary and architecture,
for the admiration of after-ages ; but the means by
which it was accomplished inflicted misery and death
upon other parts of Greece, as well as upon Athens
herself.   Possibly a Republican or any other party
in power might attempt such a scheme of plunder
and luxury in our country, but no other but a
Democratic chief with a Democratic party at his
back is likely to attempt it, or, if attempted, would

stand one chance in a hundred, as compared with a Democratic chief, of bringing the inevitable result of extravagance and disaster upon the people.

But we must close this sketch of the Greek Democracy. It is true that, by an alliance with Persia, her old enemy, Athens was able to throw off the Spartan yoke. But her political greatness and power were gone forever; and although she was able to re-establish her General Assembly of Five Thousand, it was, as before, nothing but a stage upon which her orators could spout and boast of their patriotism and valor, and through which the most adroit of her demagogues could become despotic chiefs whose patriotism consisted mainly in keeping alive their state-sovereignty theory, which continued to keep the Greek states at logger-heads with each other for fifty-five or sixty years thereafter, or until Philip of Macedon gathered all of them into his military net, to be handed over to Alexander, his son. All this was accomplished despite Demosthenes, Athens' last and greatest orator, who, after vainly striving to rally his countrymen to the defence of liberty and union, finally seeing that all was lost, died by his own hand, at the altar of his country's religion.

And here I affectionately call the attention of our Democratic brethren to this last paragraph which is for their special benefit. The word Democracy, as we have seen, was of Greek origin ; the word Republicanism, of Roman origin. The use of the two words as expressive of political systems in the world was contemporaneous, or nearly so. The history also of the Greeks and Romans was mainly contemporaneous.

The countries of the two nations were similar in climate, features, and productions. But the Romans, under Republicanism, arose from a low estate to be a great nation, and continued in that greatness, under Republican form of government, five hundred years, and became the most powerful people upon the face of the earth. Under the Democracy, the Greeks, a brilliant and highly intellectual people, flourished in greatness about one hundred years—that is, from the overthrow of the Pisistratidæ to the fall of Athens, or only eighty-five years, if we count from the battle of Marathon to the fall of Athens; which period, in fact, includes all that is counted great and grand under the reign of Democracy in Greece, unless constant internecine commotions and wars can be counted as greatness. It is true, Republicanism in Rome, at the end of five hundred years, was superseded by an empire which ruled the world six hundred years longer, but Democracy in Greece, and the people whose virtues it turned into vices, sank into abject slavery under the Philip and Alexander dynasty, and thence into slavery still more abject under the Romans, and soon thereafter into the oblivion of the grave. From the days of Republicanism in Rome to these days, the word has lived as a system and expression of human rights throughout the world, and has been applied to many nations as the synonym of their government and institutions. From the days of Democratic Greece, for the space of more than two thousand years, so far as history informs us, no people used or applied the word Democracy as a political name or system, or as the synonym of liberty, equal rights, or any other moral or political virtues among mankind.   Democracy among the Romans was known as Agrarianism, and is so regarded at the present time by nineteen twentieths of mankind.

/

CHAPTER VII.

BEFORE proceeding to the history of Democracy in modern times, it is fit and proper to seek to draw some further moral and political lessons from what we know of Greek Democracy.

As remarked in a previous chapter, it is a noteworthy fact in history, that after the fall of Democracy in Greece, the word, as a party name, or government name, was not revived by any people, so far as we are informed, for the space of two thousand years. It is also a noteworthy fact that while the literature, the arts, including the moral and mental philosophy of the ancient Greeks, have been preserved in great perfection, their political economy, and especially the principles of Democracy as a system of government, were not discussed ; or if discussed, were not preserved, unless we except and accept the writings of Plato and Aristotle, both of whom lived and wrote, the former after the fall of Athens, and the latter in the days of Macedonian despotism, and neither of whom have left any approval of Democracy as a form of government. There must, therefore, be several potent reasons for the brilliancy of the Greeks in literature and arts, and for their silence on the side

49

of political economy. Some of these reasons are herein given for the enlightenment of our modern Democrats, and for what they may be worth.

First, the disreputable origin and uncertain meaning of the word Democracy, in all its bearings and relations. Second, the demoralizing and disorganizing influence which it always exercised upon society in whatever form it was used. Third, the utter moral and political wreck to which it led the Greeks, and all other civilized people who adopted it as a political system.

We also alluded to Rome and its Republicanism, which continued to prevail in that country for five hundred years, and now we add that when the empire had taken the place of the republic, the government, out of respect to the work that Republicanism had accomplished, was for several centuries still called a republic. And when the fall of the empire took place, after six hundred years of its existence, and the people in different parts of the world were left free to form independent governments of their own, numerous communities used the word Republic as the name of their governments. Such was the case with the little republic of San Marino, the republic of Genoa, the republic of Milan, the republic of Florence, the republic of Venice, and lastly, the republic of Switzerland, to say nothing of the republics that have sprung up on the American continent. The reason for this difference and distinction in point of popularity, fame, and usage, in favor of Republicanism, is and must be that the word had a reputable origin, a certainty of meaning, and that it secured to the people order and well-regulated liberty, and had an excellent moral influence wherever it was applied as a political name.

In view, then, of the difference in the meaning, history, and fame of the two words, and before proceeding to the history of Democracy in our country, it may not be improper to propound to our modern Democratic fellow-citizens a few interrogatories, and to urge upon them the propriety of answering them at a period as early as practicable. If they should look upon these questions as a sort of political catechism which they dislike to study, they ought to write such a one for the Republicans, for the benefit of all parties, obligating themselves at the same time to answer the following questions. From such cross-examination much more good might arise than from baseless charges and the denial of the truth.

First, then, was there ever a political party formed under the name of Democracy that did not convey to the minds of its friends and its foes, the learned and the unlearned, the virtuous and the depraved, the idea that its tendency and intention were to gather into its ranks the discontented and dissolute, the depraved and the dangerous portion of society, as its chief strength and support?

Second, was there ever a party formed under this name that did not convey to its friends and its foes, the learned and the unlearned, the virtuous and the depraved, the idea that it was intended to pull down those in influence and authority, however sound in principle, however pure and patriotic they might be, and substitute in their places such leaders as would pander to the worst passions, prejudices, and appetites of human nature ?

Third, was there ever a party formed under this name which was not ready, whenever it could find a suitable leader, to plunge the community into disorder and revolution, either with or without a sufficient cause ?

Fourth, was there ever a Democratic party in possession of supreme power for a single decade, that did not produce, or attempt to produce, a revolution in the state, however sound that state's policy and constitution might be ?

Fifth, was there ever a party under the name of Democracy, which succeeded in gaining supreme power, that did not when out of power leave the state in a far worse condition than when it gained control over it, if, indeed, it had not plunged the state into civil or some other dangerous war ?

Sixth, was there ever a Democratic party that did not when in possession of supreme power keep the state in social strife, or develop a despotic leader, whom it blindly followed in trampling down liberty and equal rights, until some great catastrophe was the result ?

Seventh, was there ever a well-organized Democratic party which was not opposed in its practices, if not in its theory, to the purity and integrity of the elective franchise, and that did not gravitate to the utter subversion of this great and fundamental principle of a representative form of government ?

Eighth, was there ever a Democratic party on the face of the earth that did not cherish and uphold

the slavery of some portion of the people, and glory
in the overthrow and ostracism of the great and
good men of the land ?

, Ninth, has not Democracy, as a party name and
organization, been more prolific of despotism and
oppression in free states than any and all other
parties ever heard of ?

Tenth, was it not Democracy, in spirit and
methods, that laid the foundation for the overthrow
of the free governments of ancient times ?

Eleventh, has not a Democratic party, in spirit and
methods, if not in name, been the most reliable and
powerful ally of despotism in all ages and in all parts
of the world ?

Twelfth, was it not a Democratic party or Agrarianism, as Democracy was called in Rome, in spirit
and methods, rather than Republicanism, that enabled
Cæsar and Antony to overthrow the liberties of
Rome, and change it into an empire? Read Antony's funeral oration, and Louis Napoleon's history of
Cæsar, for an answer.

All these interrogatories are susceptible of direct
answers from history, and by any one who is but
superficially acquainted with the annals of nations
and of governments. But there are a few more questions in theory and the natural relations of mankind,
which are necessary to complete this comprehensive
catechism, here subjoined for the consideration of all,
whether Democrats or Republicans, Whigs or Tories,
loyal or disloyal men.

Thirteenth, is not human nature, in its natural
state, lamentably vile, suggesting to the mental

vision the truth of the orthodox tenet of "total depravity," and the truth of King David's suspicion that "all men are liars," and that Democracy lives and thrives upon this depravity rather than upon truth and virtue?

Fourteenth, or if you demur at this old-fashioned doctrine, which has stood the test of four thousand years, will you not confess that at least one half of the human family are in their hearts very wicked, and that a Democratic party lives and thrives upon this depravity and weakness of human nature?

Fifteenth, do we not all know that numerous communities which have stood high in civilization, learning, virtue, and intelligence, have, for the want of a firm and vigorous government, been deprived of civil liberty, and have been precipitated into despotism or mobs, which only ended in their destruction?

Sixteenth, has not a Democratic party always been the hot-bed of political vagaries, and treasonable schemes against rational liberty, and equal rights, such as Agrarianism, Jacobinism, Communism, Chartism, and Nihilism?

Seventeenth, are there not several communities, large and small, in our country at the present time, where the people are upon the verge of anarchy, where human life is as cheap and as readily taken as that of a cat or a dog, and is not this state of affairs directly or indirectly traceable to a Democratic party, and the disintegrating and anarchical sentiments it propagates?

Eighteenth, and if these and hundreds of other

vices inseparable from a Democratic party, and hundreds of calamities have been the outgrowth of a Democratic party in possession of supreme power, what evils may we not expect from such a party in such a country as ours, when our population is increased two, three, or fivefold, and the temptations to anarchy and crime are vastly augmented?

Nineteenth, has not free government, rational liberty, and equal rights ever been the most difficult problem to solve, the most difficult work to accomplish ever undertaken by mankind? And does not such a government, such labor, such liberty, such rights, require that the most intelligent and virtuous portion of the people, as measured by Christian principles and precepts, bear sway rather than the most ignorant and depraved portion, such as but too frequently predominate in a Democratic party?

Twentieth, are not the liberties and equal rights of the people, and the safety and security of any country, more perfect and complete without a Democratic party than with one?

Twenty-first, has any Democratic party in possession of supreme power ever wrought out or conferred any substantial benefit on any people or country?

Twenty-second, has any Democratic party ever been known to extend or enlarge the area of liberty and equal rights, or remove the shackles of slavery from any people or country?

Twenty-third, has any Democratic party once in possession of supreme power ever been known to yield up such power, without plunging the country into a bloody and cruel war of some kind?

When these interrogatories are fully and fairly answered, it will be a good time for some one to make a history for the friends of Democracy. Or when our Democratic leaders can give us the history of a Democratic party that has not been distinguished for the vices and calamities implied in these interrogatories, our present Democratic party will be entitled to prepare a catechism for the Republican or any other political party, seeking to mount into supreme power.

CHAPTER VIII.

THE first great political parties in this country
were the Whigs and Tories, which sprang up previous
to the Revolutionary War, and which continued
to its close. The Whigs were the friends and
advocates of independence, and the Tories were its
opponents, and fought against independence and
home government to the close of the war. The first
Democratic party in this country sprang into existence at or near the close of the Revolutionary
struggle, and "with charity for all and malice
toward none," it is our duty to inform the reader
that this first Democratic party in America was comprised mainly of the Tories, and such other men
as naturally fall into a disintegrating and anarchical
party wherever one is found. It may be true,
that for two or three years after the Revolutionary
War was over, party lines were not sharply defined,
or their principles fully developed. Yet the
Whigs were the fast, firm friends of independence
and a firm national government from the beginning,
while the Tory Democrats were always and everywhere conspicuous as the opponents of these great
American principles, using their influence and means
to keep the country first under the British yoke,
and failing in that, under the hackle of state

sovereignty and anarchy, and finally animated by a
desire to throw the country back under the control
of Great Britain, or some other European government. And, strange as it may seem to us of the
present day, this Democratic party first gained
formidable proportions and strength in the two great
States of Virginia and Massachusetts. From these
two great commonwealths, the Democratic party
soon spread out and over other States, upsetting
not only old English forms and customs, but upsetting and deranging all laws and civilized progress, as all Democratic parties have an unfortunate
aptness for doing.

This early Democratic party first directed its
powers against the improvement and settlement of
the State constitutions, by opposing two houses in
the legislative bodies, by the curtailment of the
salaries and the time of holding offices, but more
notably by filling legislative assemblies with dissolute, ignorant, and wild characters, but more especially by the undermining and disintegration of the
national Congress and a national form of government. As is well known, the first Congress, or
national government consisted of only one assembly,
chosen at first by the people in the respective States
and districts, and although this was the case, the first
assembly assumed and exercised in the name of the
people the customary and time-honored national
powers. This was called the Revolutionary Congress, and did its work with energy and fidelity. But
it was not long before the Democratic spirit, which
soon ripened into a Democratic party and filled the

State Legislatures with wild and reckless men, filled the Congress of the United States with men of its own way of thinking, and these in turn soon trampled down and out all the powers that the first Congress had assumed and exercised, and so continued to do, until the government itself had become utterly imbecile, and the country was in great confusion, distress, and anarchy. This we shall more clearly see as we proceed with our sketches, which are written for the consideration of hard-working and honest people, rather than for the learned and ambitious politicians, who know all these things, but prefer to keep the people in darkness about them.

As just remarked, this Democratic distemper, for so it may be called, first broke out in Massachusetts, and showed itself in the form of complaints against the high salary of the governor and other officials. It next attacked the State Senate, as being a superfluous branch of the government. In the next place it claimed that the State ought to issue treasury notes, or, as we would say nowadays, greenbacks and fiat money, in such quantities that every man might have plenty. Upon these issues, the party set on foot a civil war called Shay's Insurrection, and put into the field about fifteen hundred men, who, after committing robberies and various other crimes, were met by an equal number of loyal citizens, well armed, and after the fall of ten or fifteen Democrats, they were scattered to the four winds, never again to assemble, at least up to the present time, to threaten the government of that State.

" 'T is true, and pity 't is 't is true," that Democracy

next broke out in Virginia, and raged with great violence in that State for many, many years. It is well
known that Virginia, previous to the Revolution,
had been under the influence and control of a quasi-
aristocracy, similar in spirit and influence to the aristocracy of England, but which, under the leadership
of Thomas Jefferson, had been torn up by the roots,
but unfortunately the counteraction was too sudden
to be healthy. It gave the power of the State into
the hands of a class of people headed by demagogues calling themselves Democrats, which class,
when organized, or rather when fired up with Democratic notions, would have done credit to an Athenian rabble in the days of Clisthenes, and would
probably, with such a leader, have trampled the
elective franchise in the dust. John Marshall, who
was afterward Chief-Justice of the United States,
said " the people of Virginia idolized Democracy."
Certain it is that it took so deep root among them
that it has had control of the State from that day to
this, and, viewed from a human standpoint, it came
very near preventing the ratification of our great
charter of union, domestic tranquillity, common defence, general welfare, and liberty to ourselves and
our posterity ; and despite the conservative power of
this charter and her many great men, it kept the
State in a deplorably dilapidated condition, until the
Democrats finally took up arms against the constitution and government of their fathers.

    To form some idea of the demoralization of the
people under this early Democracy, and the consequent character and impotence of the government

of the State, the following extract is taken from a speech of Governor Edmund Randolph delivered in the Virginia Convention of 1788, called to ratify the great Federal charter. After giving a graphic account of the horrid state of morals, commerce, industry, and manners, he said :—"A man who was a citizen was deprived of his life thus: From mere reliance on general reports, a gentleman in the House of Delegates informed the House that a certain man (Joseph Phillips) had committed several crimes, and was running at large perpetrating other crimes. He therefore moved for leave to attaint him. He obtained that leave instantly, and drawing a bill from his pocket it was read three times in one day and carried to the Senate. He was attainted speedily and precipitately, without any proof better than vague reports, without being confronted with his accusers and witnesses, without the privilege of calling for evidence in his behalf. He was sentenced to death, and was afterward actually executed."

No one who is able to read and appreciate this piece of history can fail to be struck with the deplorable condition of the then great State of Virginia, or to see that it had arisen in the main from the baleful excitement of the word Democracy as a party name and influence.

The moral and political condition of the other States was similar to these leading ones, except Rhode Island, where the Democracy had actually ripened into an oligarchy, which for a long time held sway in the State, and prevented the ratification of the Constitution of the United States therein for

three years after it had been presented to the people
by the Federal Convention, and until the General
Government was about to put its foot on its Democratic, oligarchic, and aristocratic neck.

As touching this state of affairs in the country,
Mr. John Adams, the first Vice-President and the
second President under the new Constitution, said:
" Negligence of its (the Constitution's) regulations, in-
attention to its recommendations, if not disobedience
to its authority, not only in individuals but in States,
soon appeared, with their melancholy consequences :
universal languor, jealousies and rivalries of the
States, decline of navigation and commerce, dis-
couragement of necessary manufactures, universal
fall in the value of lands and their products, contempt of public and private faith, loss of consideration and credit with foreign nations, and at length
in discontents, animosities, and combinations, partial
conventions and insurrections, threatening some
great national calamity.

" In this dangerous crisis the American people
were not abandoned by their usual good sense, presence of mind, resolution, and integrity." . . .
And he might have added : Which, together with the
blessing of God, preserved from utter ruin all that
the fathers had achieved.

Mr. James Madison, the fourth President, on one
occasion, alluding to the same state of affairs, said:
" As a natural consequence of this distracted and
disheartening condition of the Union, the Federal
authority had ceased to be respected abroad, and
dispositions were shown there, particularly in Great

Britain, to take advantage of its imbecility, and to speculate on its approaching downfall. At home it had lost all confidence and credit, the unstable and unjust career of the States had also forfeited the respect and confidence essential to order and good government, involving a general decay of confidence and credit between man and man."

That the Democracy of those days had greatly demoralized the good-sense, presence of mind, resolution, and integrity of the people, spoken of by Mr. Adams, and that it had brought all the disorder and ruin upon the country of which Mr. Adams and Mr. Madison speak, and that the Democracy was then opposed to a firm national government, and that its leaders did all they could to defeat the Constitution, there is no ground of doubt. In the discussion of the Constitution in the Federal Convention, and especially upon the question of electing the representatives in Congress by the people, instead of the State governments, the Democracy was alluded to as an objection and argument against the former method. Edmund Randolph, in the Federal Convention, said : " He deplored the turbulence and follies of the Democracy." Mr. Madison also, who was then counted a Democrat, complained of " the oppression and injustice experienced from the Democracy." Mr. George Mason, another Democratic delegate from Virginia, " admitted the danger of Democracy." Alexander Hamilton, although in favor of electing the representatives in Congress by the people, said : " He was alarmed by the amazing violence and turbulence of the Democratic spirit."

Elbridge Gerry said : " The Democrats do not want
virtue, but are the dupes of pretended patriots."
And again, he said : " It would seem to be a maxim
of the Democracy to starve the public servants."
And still again, in his State, he thought " Democracy the worst of all political evils."

It is rather heart-rending to make these historical
revelations about our Democratic brethren.   It
would be much pleasanter to offer them more
palatable and delightful reading, but as good citizens
and patriots they should bear in mind that, if the
party should ever again come into power, as it ex-
pects to do soon, these developments may, in such
a fearful contingency, operate as reminders of their
faults, their weak and bad points, and thereby put
them on their good behavior, and possibly save
them and their country from the ruin which a Democratic party in power has always heretofore brought
upon the people.

CHAPTER IX.

THOMAS JEFFERSON NOT A DEMOCRAT.—DEMOCRACY
CLASSIFIED.—THE DECLARATION OF INDEPENDENCE NOT
A DEMOCRATIC DOCUMENT.—THE ARTICLES OF CONFED-
ERATION PURELY DEMOCRATIC.—THE CONSTITUTION
OF THE UNITED STATES PROVIDENTIALLY RATIFIED BY
THE PEOPLE, REGARDLESS OF DEMOCRACY.

IT is a sad, a very sad piece of business, to upset
the consolation and comfort that our modern Democratic brethren have enjoyed in the belief that
Thomas Jefferson was a Democrat. But truth, fair-
ness, and good-fellowship demand that it should be
done. It is true enough that Jefferson was called a
radical, a disorganizer in politics, and did many very
naughty things that looked like Democratic deeds,
and hence it is, we suppose, that many modern Democrats claim him as a man after their own hearts.
Yet he was not a Democrat in name, spirit, or practice. His biographer says "he was a Republican and
a philanthropist," and that "the term Democracy
was seldom used or countenanced by him." In his
first inaugural address as President of the United
States he said: "We are all Republicans and we
are all Federalists," meaning by the term Republicans his own friends and party, and by Federalists
the party of Washington, Adams, and Hamilton.
It is well known that he always repelled the term

Democracy, when applied to him and his party by the Federalists, and that his entire administration of eight years was as far from the instincts and practices of Democracy as that of Washington, unless his bold assumptions of power may be called Democracy.

It would make this volume too long to undertake a detailed account of the demoralization and disorders that took place in various parts of the country as the result of wild and rabid Democratic notions during the years preceding the adoption of the Constitution. The idea of Democracy known as State Sovereignty was most conspicuous, and played a part almost as pernicious as idolatry played among the Israelites after the death of Joshua.

Yet the Democracy, as a party, as was the case with it in ancient Greece, and as it ever has been with it in this country, was opposed to a "firm, national government." But at that time, disorder and lawlessness were wide-spread, threatening civil war, or some other formidable evil, greatly exciting and alarming the people. As a consequence, the State governments, though Democratic, were compelled to take some action, looking toward a national organization. These governments, therefore, proceeded to appoint delegates to the national convention to assemble in Philadelphia. But true to the Democratic instinct, to hold to power as long as practicable, they stipulated in appointing these delegates, that, first, the work of the convention should be confined to amendments of the old Articles of Confederation ; and second, that the suggestions the convention might make should be referred back to the State governments, rather than to the people, for ratification or rejection. It is also worthy of note, that these State governments in appointing delegates, in order to shield themselves as much as possible from responsibility of the proposed innovation as they called it, took care to select nearly all from the old Whigs and anti-Democrats. This selection might be regarded as an interposition of Divine Providence—who holds the affairs of nations in the hollow of His hand and brings to naught the designs of those who oppose His plans—for the redemption of the people, in the same manner that Providence afterward made use of a Democratic war for the perpetuation of slavery, as a means to free the colored people from their bonds.

But before proceeding farther on this line of history, we must go back to a point when Democracy had not made its appearance in our country ; namely, to the commencement of the Revolutionary war.

And here too we may remark that many persons suppose that the people and the Democracy were the same, and that the two words when used as political terms mean the same thing. This is a great mistake. The word people, whether used socially, politically, or numerically, means the entire citizenship, the rich and the poor, the learned and the unlearned, the young and the old, the laity and the clergy, those in office and those out of office. The Democracy means everywhere, and on all occasions, a class, or a political party, composed in the main of the ignorant, the dissolute, and the discontented, who are always so defined and addressed by their leaders and spokesmen,

and who are always appealed to as the oppressed
portion of society, whether there are any grounds for
such complaint or not, whether the other portion of
society is doing all it can for their elevation and
happiness or not; that is to say, they are so appealed
to if they are freemen with votes at their command,
but if they are slaves, no word of complaint is ever
uttered by a Democratic leader in their favor.   In
the nature of things, the Democracy cannot mean the
learned, the moral, and intellectual portion of society.
Charles Dickens is said to have been a great friend
of the poor, the weak, and the lowly, but he was
never counted a Democrat.   Socrates was counted a
great friend of the poor and humble, but he was
never counted a Democrat; but among the ancient
Greeks, Clisthenes, Pericles, and Alcibiades were
Democrats, and were great Democratic leaders, who
seem to have depended mainly on the dissolute and
ignorant portions of society for power and support.
In our country, Patrick Henry and Luther Martin
were counted Democrats and representatives of the
Democratic spirit.   In France, Danton, Marat, and
Robespierre were representatives of the Democratic
party of their day and country.   Napoleon Bonaparte was at first a Democrat, and whether so or not
when he seized upon imperial power, he always relied
upon the Democratic element for power and support.
But no one supposes that all the Greek people, all
the French people, or all the American people were
ever Democrats.   Unquestionably there have been
more people in all civilized countries who favored
and upheld freedom and liberty for all, and who never

embraced Democratic sentiments, or believed in a Democratic party, than were ever found in Democratic ranks. Indeed, we do not read of any Democratic party that ever abolished or opposed slavery. Hence we come to the conclusion that the Democracy never meant the same thing as the people, or the people the same thing as the Democracy.

The Revolutionary Congress, which assembled in Philadelphia in 1774, was composed of men and patriots appointed by the people in their primary assemblies, and represented all conditions of people. A Democratic party had not then arisen, and had no part or lot in the movement. The powers that this first Congress exercised were assumed in their representative capacity as the powers of the people and as afterward expressed in the Declaration of Independence. The powers that this first Congress exercised were supreme, as they should have been, and partook of sovereign authority, such as obtains in all legitimate national governments. For two years, and until after the Declaration of Independence, there was no hesitancy or question among the people of the supreme character and authority of the Congress. It is true this Congress did not constitute a perfect and complete system of government, but it did not shrink from acts or measures which were demanded by the exigencies of the occasion, as the history of those years fully demonstrates.

But alas for those days! when the great sovereign act of independence had been put forth, and the great work of the war had hardly begun, these representatives of the people called a halt, and instead of forming, as they could and should have done, a complete national government, they conceived the crude, and almost fatal idea that the newly declared States, with their crude and half-formed governments, could and would perform this great work—a work, by the way, which none but despotic power, or the people, in their primary and representative capacity, have ever been able to perform. Out of this omission to form a suitable government, which the clangor of war would have sanctioned, State sovereignty arose with its hydra-heads, and Democracy soon began to show its teeth, claws, and glaring eyeballs on every occasion. After years of labor, and days and nights of prayer and supplication to these State governments, by good and patriotic men, to consent to a suitable form of national government, the result was the Articles of Confederation, with these truly Democratic words emblazoned upon its front: " Each State retains its sovereignty, freedom, and independence," which, of course, placed a veto power in the hands of each State, and soon reduced what remained of a national government to a nullity, and society to the condition already described. But, fortunately, to again repeat the words of John Adams: " In this dangerous crisis, the American people were not abandoned by their usual good-sense, presence of mind, resolution, and integrity," nor indeed by the presence and blessing of God.

And again, in this dangerous crisis, the delegates, who had been appointed by the State governments, learning wisdom from the omissions of the Revolutionary Congress, and not being willing to commit another great mistake, took the ship of state into their own hands, regardless of the instructions of the State governments, and framed a complete and thorough national Constitution, providing for its submission to the votes of the people for ratification, rather than to the State governments. This great charter of union, justice tranquillity, common defence, general welfare, and liberty, was thus ratified by an overwhelming majority of the people's votes.

And now, in closing this chapter, it is a sad thing for our Democratic brethren of to-day for it to be said that the opponents of the Constitution of 1789 were unquestionably Democrats in spirit, words, and acts, if not in name and organization, and that so great were the demoralization, disorder, and distress of the people, and so great were the demoralization and weakness of the State governments and the courts, as the consequence of Democratic sentiments and methods, and so thoroughly had the people been scourged by Democracy during the thirteen years from the Declaration of Independence to the adoption of the Constitution of 1789, that the word Democracy, as a party name and organization, became odious, and disappeared, as such, for the next forty years. And in all this we again see the hand of a kind and protecting Providence.

It is not strange that Thomas Jefferson declined to be called a Democrat.

CHAPTER X.

As related in the foregoing chapters, upon the adoption of the great charter of liberty, and the reconstruction of the government under it in 1789, Democracy, as a party name and organization, disappeared from the country, except so far as the old Whigs and the Constitutional party applied the term to their opponents as a term of reproach. But as darkness is opposed to light, and as the negative is sometimes as valuable for illustration as the affirmative, and as the pestilence is better understood when it is past and gone than when present, so are bad political principles better understood when their consequences have been experienced.

In the absence, then, of the Democratic party, the new Constitution being accepted as the fundamental law of the country, "the great experiment of testing the plan," as Patrick Henry said, "was to take place." This great work, as a matter of course, demanded a large amount of wisdom, a large amount of labor, ingenuity, and patriotic devotion. Almost every part of the Constitution, almost every relation and interest of society, as a nation, as well as the internal interests and relations of the country, required numerous measures, numerous agencies, to regulate and protect these interests. Owing to the reactionary and disturbing tactics of the early Democrats, the work was slow and difficult, and even dangerous. Almost the first measure was that of raising revenue for the use of the government—a task always difficult and delicate, but now rendered more so than usual from the utter failure of the Democratic Articles of Confederation at this very point. Next came the means and methods of furnishing a medium of commercial operations and exchanges, both paper and metallic, both for the use of the people and the government itself. Owing to the scarcity of gold and silver in the country, and the sad experience the people had had with paper money, this measure was beset by difficulties and dangers, but the vast surplus products of the country—*in prospectu*—and the vast fields of foreign commerce inviting enterprise, prevented the government from neglecting to provide for the life-blood of industry and trade. Next came the Post-office Department, with all its extended branches, and with all its necessary and complicated parts, comprising a vast piece of machinery in which every living soul had an immediate and direct interest at stake. Next came the Department of War, and eventually a Navy, for protection against internal and external foes, all of which vast amount of machinery, with its details, was constructed and put into operation in the absence, and without the interference, of an organized Democratic party ; but God only knows how it could have been done in the presence of such a party, and against the instincts it always has had for obstruction and ruin.

But it was not long before the young government

had to contend with insurrections and threatened insurrections, springing from the smouldering embers of the defunct Democratic party. It also had Indian wars on its hands, and obstructions and threatening troubles with the Spaniards, who held the mouth of the Mississippi River. It also soon had a war, or a difficulty—if possible worse than a war —with France, its old ally, augmented greatly, as we shall presently see, by surviving Democratic spirits. All this took place within the first few years, and all was surmounted, and the integrity and honor of the government preserved and maintained, in the absence of a Democratic party, and despite its lingering propensities and love of confusion.

And here, for the purpose of continuing our thread of history and the enlightenment of our Democratic brethren, it should be remarked that out of this difficulty with France, namely, the audacious and insulting interference of the then Democratic French Government with the rights and prerogatives of our government on our own soil, and the capture of our shipping on the high seas, grew the "Alien and Sedition Laws," on the part of our government, for its own protection and defence, about which rivers of filthy Democratic ink and crocodile tears have been shed. Necessary and proper as these laws were in the distressed condition of our country, they were seized upon, not only for abuse of their authors, but as a pretext for the seditious and treasonable Democratic Kentucky resolutions, which may now be considered as an utterance of the slumbering Democratic party. These resolutions were, as a matter of course, in strong sympathy with the French Democracy and its bloody work, and about which no Democratic penitential ink or tears have been shed from that day to this.

It is not for the writer of these papers, or for any other person of to-day, to portray the motives of Mr. Jefferson in writing these resolutions, except to say he virtually denied their authorship for twenty years, and thus recognized by his denial their treasonable character, which the whole world, except the Democrats, stamped upon them. But be this as it may, it is proper here to speak a little further upon the character of the Alien and Sedition Laws, and to say, as we may with truth, at this day, that these laws were emphatically war measures, well suited to meet the audacious conduct of the French Democratic emissaries who were opening in this country, in defiance of our government, recruiting offices for their own army, and who were fitting out armed vessels in our ports to make war upon a nation with whom the United States were at peace, while the French navy were capturing and confiscating our mercantile ships. Nor was the capture of our shipping and these violations under the nose of our government of neutral rights, all that was being done by the French to insult us. They started Democratic newspapers in our cities, among which was one called the *Aurora*, in Philadelphia, the vilest of the vile, and all filled with such coarse and scurrilous articles against the President and the government of our country, as none but French Democrats schooled in the society of Marat,

Danton, and Robespierre, could write, and none but Democrats with the vilest of appetites could swallow.

It was against these acts and provocations, and such others as French Democrats alone could invent, and in view of the imminent danger of having French Democratic atrocities re-enacted in our own country, that the Alien and Sedition Laws were enacted by the Congress of the United States. The wonder is, and long has been, with all honest men, why it was that, instead of these mild measures, our government did not apprehend and imprison or hang these Democratic emissaries, instead of treating them as mildly as it did. And here it should be stated, for the information of our Democratic fellow-citizens of to-day, so atrocious were these French acts that more than thirty years after their occurrence Andrew Jackson, the first genuine Democratic President of this country, was exceedingly anxious to make war upon the French on account of them, and because the French Government refused to pay damages for the same.

It may be repeated, therefore, that the time has come when, in giving a sketch of Democracy, as a party name and organization in our country, these Alien and Sedition Laws should be frankly and openly defended before all American readers, and when, if they are to be condemned at all, it should be for their mildness and clemency, rather than for their severity, under the great provocation. The Alien and Sedition Laws, with all the condemnation that the Democracy of this country has been able to heap upon them were right, and more especially on the Alien Law, stands at this day upon the statute-books of the country as the law of the land, notwith-standing the fact that the Democratic party of this country has had the control and direction of the government for more than thirty years since that time without attempting its repeal. The Sedition Law was but a temporary measure, having been enacted for three years, and having expired of its own limitation, after some two or three traitors had been arrested under it, and held as prisoners for a short time.

Such, it may be repeated, were the Alien and Se-dition Laws, which were made a pretext for the truly seditious and treasonable Democratic " Kentucky Resolutions," and which have been a sweet morsel under Democratic tongues until "State-sovereignty" sentiments culminated in the great Democratic Rebel-lion. And here it may be mentioned that these laws enacted by the party of Washington, Adams, and Hamilton, have been made the target and the topic of more Democratic hypocritical cant, and more Democratic lying literature than was ever heard of or drawn from any other subject, and which, in fact, if reproduced in newspaper form, we may suppose would shingle the country from Passammaquoddy to the Golden Gate, and from the Lakes to the Gulf of Mexico: the material would, it is true, be filthy, and if lifted into the air by a very strong wind, might so darken the earth and so blind and disgust the angels of light as to cause them to turn their faces from our country forever. For eighty long

years these laws have served as a cloak and a
shelter, from behind which Democrats have been
accustomed to blacken the character and stab the
reputation of every great and pure patriot of the
country from Washington down to the present day.

Mr. Jefferson may have written the Kentucky
resolutions for partisan and peaceful purposes only.
He certainly had too much sense to suppose
that these Alien and Sedition Laws, enacted as war
measures, had in them any danger to the country,
the Constitution, or civil liberty. If he prepared
the resolutions for disunion and treasonable purposes,
his patriotism must have been very much improved
by his election to the Presidency; and as he did
not use in them the terms Democracy or State sovereignty, we suppose the mantle of charity should be
cast over his fame and name.

CHAPTER XI.

WE must now come to the consideration of the first fully organized, armed, and equipped Democratic party in this country, and a series of reactionary movements, and the most surprising and inconsistent Revolution, that ever took place in any country in time of profound peace, and such a reaction and Revolution as never could have taken place, from good to bad, in any civilized and enlightened community, except as a consequence of the accession to supreme power of a Democratic, or some equally wild and reckless party. Perhaps it is too early by a generation or two for the entire people of this country to see and fully appreciate the terrible evils that came from the administrations of Andrew Jackson and Martin Van Buren, and the wicked counsels which guided them. But it is not too early for each and every lover of his country to recount these evils, and to seek to warn his countrymen against the recurrence of such.

Perhaps we should not neglect to observe that there are many good men who call themselves Democrats, who, in State and other local matters, act wisely as public servants. It is also probable that even the political partisans acting under the

Constitution and laws of the United States, which constitute nine tenths of the points and rules by which their actions are guided and controlled, and through which every intelligent man can understand what ought and what ought not to be done by the local governments, need not be impugned as to their patriotism or right-doing. But when such a party, a party mainly composed, themselves being judges, of the ignorant and the depraved of all classes, assumes national proportions, to the exclusion of the intelligent, virtuous, and wise portion of society, and, to the exclusion also, if you please, of the rich, and this element of theirs comprises the preponderating element in the party, and this party gains possession of supreme, national power, the whole political and moral aspect of the community becomes changed, and the ship of state is soon driven, without compass or chart, among rocks and quicksands, until a wreck ensues. For indeed such a party, in possession of supreme power, dealing with measures which not one in a thousand can fully comprehend, knows and can know no precedent and no rule of action for its course and conduct, but its own ambition and its own passions, as will be shown was the case during the times of which we are about to speak. Nor can this historical sketch fail to demonstrate the force and truth of the proverb, "when the righteous are in authority the people rejoice, but when the wicked bear rule the people mourn."

It is well known to all who are familiar with the political history of this country, that at the

time of Gen. Jackson's elevation to the Presidency
in 1829, the people were in the most prosperous condition they ever had been since they had achieved
their independence.   The great New York and
Erie Canal had been completed; the Pennsylvania
and the Baltimore and Ohio canals were being pushed
toward the Western States, so that the products of
the Western plains were already conveyed by these
routes to and along the Atlantic coast.   The Mississippi River, its branches, and the lakes had been
covered with steamers carrying to and fro, and tow-
ing immense barges loaded with mineral and agricultural products of all kinds.   Manufacturing establishments East and West, North and South,
were being started, and were everywhere profitable and prosperous.   Mechanics and laborers of
every kind found abundant employment at high
wages.   Thousands of men were flocking westward
to get themselves homes upon government lands,
and to become wealthy by their industry and enterprise, as thousands did, before the country was
struck by the great Democratic cyclone and the
moral contagion that followed.   The railway and
locomotive had already been invented and were
being constructed.   The hopes and expectations
from these new inventions were very great, and men
were looking forward to the national and State
governments to aid in driving them over or through
the Alleghany Mountains from the East and South
to the great Northwest.   We may add that the
culture of cotton was rapidly on the increase in
the South.

The country had then been at peace with all the European powers for fifteen years, and under such rulers as James Madison, James Monroe, and John Quincy Adams, the people had enjoyed the benefit of wise and prudent legislation on the part of the general government, and especially in the great measures of revenue, a tariff with protection for home industry, and a prudent and safe system of internal improvements by Congress, all of which co-operated to give a powerful impetus to industry and enterprise of every kind. In addition to these a national bank, with twenty-five branches in the leading cities and sections, had been established. This gave additional stimulus to industry and enterprise, while it also provided a sound currency, cheap exchange, and safe places of deposit for the government and the people. In a word, every branch of industry, every branch of business, every line of trade, both foreign and domestic, was in a healthy condition, and the people as a whole were buoyant, prosperous, and happy. And now, before giving the readers some contemporary testimony of the condition of the country at that time, when the Democracy commenced its overturn, I remark that notwithstanding the howling Dervishes that then arose to condemn the measures of the government, and blacken the character of the statesmen who enacted and upheld them, there is not now a sane man, or an intelligent Democrat who would dare to stand up and repeat one of the thousands of libels that were then heaped upon those measures and men who led in them, unless it be some old Nullifier who had made, without shame or reason, a great noise in South Carolina about protection.   Nor can any one at this day point to a measure that had been enacted, or that was in prospect, upon which the election of Jackson turned, unless it was the fact, as De Tocqueville expresses it, " that he was called to the 'lofty station,' by virtue of his having been commander of the American forces at the ·battle and defences of New Orleans, for which latter position he had not a single qualification."

We shall now give some cotemporary testimony, as to the condition of the country at the time of Jackson's election, the credibility of which neither Whigs nor Tories, Republicans nor Democrats, can question.   Mr. Clay, in his speech in the Senate, February, 1832, said :

" I have now to perform the more pleasing task of exhibiting an imperfect sketch of the existing state of the unparalleled prosperity of the country.   On a general survey, we behold cultivation extended, the arts flourishing, the face of the country improved, our people fully and profitably employed, and the public countenance exhibiting tranquillity, contentment, and happiness.   And if we descend into particulars we have the agreeable contemplation of a people out of debt ; land rising slowly in value, but in a secure and salutary degree ; a ready though not extravagant market for all the surplus productions of our industry ; innumerable flocks and herds bellowing and gambolling on ten thousand hills and plains, covered with rich and verdant grasses ; our cities expanded, and whole villages springing up, as it were, by enchantment; our exports and imports increased and increasing; our tonnage, foreign and coastwise, swelling and fully occupied ; the rivers of our interior animated by the perpetual thunder and lightning of countless steam-boats; the currency sound and abundant; the public debt of two wars nearly redeemed ; and, to cover all, the public treasury overflowing, embarrassing Congress, not to find subjects of taxation, but to select the objects which shall be liberated from the impost. If the term of seven years were to be selected, of the greatest prosperity which this people have enjoyed since the establishment of their present Constitution, it would be exactly that period of seven years which immediately followed the passage of the tariff of 1824."

To most men this testimony is doubtless sufficient to make clear the prosperous condition of the country. But Democrats may like some evidence from Democratic authority. We find in Jackson's first message to Congress in 1829 the following paragraphs. When these are given, and the record of his administration has been examined, we shall try to present to our readers some faint conception of the terrible wreck and horrible disasters which his administration brought upon the nation. He says :

" In communicating with you for the first time, it is to me a source of unfeigned satisfaction, calling for mutual congratulation and devout thanks to a benign Providence, that we are at peace with all mankind, and that our country exhibits the most cheering evidence of general welfare and progressive improvement."

" The public prosperity is evinced in the increased revenue arising from the sales of public lands, and in the steady maintenance of that produced by imports and tonnage, notwithstanding the additional duties imposed by the Act of 19th of May, 1828, and the usual importations in the early part of the year."

" The state of the finances exhibits the resources of the nation in an aspect highly flattering to its industry, and auspicious of the ability of the government in a very short time to extinguish the public debt."

" The balance in the treasury on the 1st of January, 1829, was five millions nine hundred and seventy-two thousand four hundred and thirty-five dollars and eighty-one cents. The receipts of the current year are estimated at twenty-four millions six hundred and two thousand two hundred and thirty dollars."

In reference to the great measures which it had taken the government nearly forty years to mature and render satisfactory to the people, on March the 4th, in his inaugural address, he said:

" Internal improvement and a diffusion of knowledge, so far as they can be promoted by constitutional acts of the Federal Government, are of high importance."

In his first annual message he says again :

" Every member of the Union in peace and in war will be benefited by the improvement of inland navigation, and the construction of highways in the several States."

And again he says :

" The general rule to be applied in graduating the duties upon articles of foreign growth and manufacture, is that which will place our own in fair competition with those of other countries, and the inducements to advance even a step beyond this point are controlling in regard to those articles which are of primary necessity in time of war."

And now as to the bank, he says:

" The charter of the Bank of the United States expires in 1836, and its stockholders will most probably apply for a renewal of their privileges. In order to avoid the evils resulting from precipitancy in a measure involving such important principles and such deep pecuniary interests, I feel that I cannot, in justice to the parties interested, too soon present it to the deliberate consideration of the Legislature and the people."

There is, there can be, no question that in these first addresses (1829) Jackson gave a candid and correct account of the condition of the people and the finances of the country, as well as a correct reflex of his own mind and the public expectations at that time, on all the great questions touched upon by him ; and that he also gave voice to the public sentiment in regard to the tariff, in regard to internal improvements, and the re-charter of the Bank of the United States, there are no grounds to doubt ; and that if he had had honest and patriotic men about him, as confidential advisers, instead of what was called a " kitchen Cabinet," comprised of a gang of political bummers, his administration might have been a benefit, rather than a scourge, to the American people.

CHAPTER XII.

IT is evident from various circumstances, and especially from the addresses of Jackson in 1829, from which the extracts in the foregoing chapter were taken, and which clearly show the prosperous condition of the country at that time, that he, Jackson, had not conceived the idea of assailing, much less the thought of destroying, the great measures and policies of the fathers of the republic. Nor is it at all probable that he then had any just conception of the nature and instincts of a genuine Democratic party, or the proclivities that such a party has always manifested for the overthrow of great and good men, and any and all measures such men have supported and upheld. But there were men, sharp and unscrupulous men, in the party, who had taken part in forming it ; men who had been foremost in traducing the great leaders of the country, whether dead or alive ; men who comprehended the situation, who understood what such a party meant, who had studied and mastered its elements and its susceptibilities, especially when in possession of supreme power. They knew that such a party always has an insatiable thirst for place and the

spoils of office, and that its chief delight is, and
always has been, in ripping up and tearing down
what has been built up, whether it be the character
of great men or the merits of great measures. And
hence, instead of being disposed to restrain or
moderate the ambition of their followers, instead of
being content to add to or improve the measures
and policies of the fathers, and thereby adapt them
to the growing interests and necessities of the country, these leaders resolved to mount the chariot of
passion and frenzy, like Phaeton of old, and drive it
with reckless speed, regardless of consequences, giving their followers no time to reflect or moderate
their views. To this end, being already in possession of the government, they assailed the great
measures and men of the country with a bitterness
and vulgarity never before known in this or any
other country since the days of Catiline, and roused
the ignorant and vicious portion of society to a
pitch of passion and prejudice such as was never
before witnessed without producing an internecine
war, and which would have produced such a war at
that time had not nearly all the virtue and intelligence of the country been found among the opponents of Democracy, and had not these opponents
chosen to suffer calumny and all sorts of wrongs,
rather than see their country deluged with fraternal
blood.

It seems at this day quite incredible that such
men as Martin Van Buren, Silas Wright, and Wm.
L. Marcy did not see and clearly understand that
the reversal of the system of internal improvements

recommended by Washington and inaugurated under
Jefferson ; the overthrow of the protective tariff,
inaugurated in the first year of Washington's administration, and approved by every President up to the
time of Jackson, and especially the overthrow of the
Bank of the United States and its twenty-five
branches, the system of which had been first inaugurated under Washington, and had been approved by
every other President, would plunge the country
into the throes of ruin and death. But fascinated
by such an apt leader and spokesman as Thos. H.
Benton, the most egotistical, vain, and pompous
man in America, they installed him as chief driver,
orator, and boss ; they mounted his chariot, they
swallowed his ribald language until his own State,
and the rank and file of Democracy throughout the
land, became sick, and spewed him out, as Democrats always do when they find a leader powerless to
feed them on spoils of office and public plunder,
which, fortunately for the country, Benton was not
always able to do.

But before proceeding to discuss further the
doings of the Democracy touching these great
measures, we must refer to another point, another
political principle, if principle it may be called,
which, it must be acknowledged, was a leading one
in the canvass that brought Jackson into the Presidency, and the only well-defined tenet of the party,
as it always has been in every Democratic party that
has ever existed,—namely, State or local sovereignty.
This dogma comprised the chief topic, and the chief
principle of the Jackson party, if any principle it

had, in the canvass which resulted in the first election
of Jackson to the Presidency. All else was calumny
and vulgar abuse of all who opposed his election to
the exalted position. Nearly all the Democratic
newspapers, and all the Democratic stumps from
Maine to Louisiana, and from the Lakes to the Capes
of Florida, resounded with this State-sovereignty
theory, and with calumny and abuse of the old
Republican and Federal leaders, all of which talk
was tipped and garnished with hypocritical cant
about the "Alien and Sedition Laws," which had
been passed thirty years before.

No one ever questioned Jackson's loyalty to the
Union or the Government of the United States, or
his skill and bravery as a soldier. But he was a man
of limited education, limited political information,
and of a stubborn and vindictive disposition. When
his mind was made up on any point, often enough
from one-sided information, however wrong or absurd the conclusion, he followed it with perti-
nacity, and became intensely bitter, dogged, and
inimical to all who opposed his views. Hence it
came to pass when he became President, after having
read the newspapers and speeches of his friends only,
and having studied their arguments in favor of State
sovereignty, we have the astounding phenomenon of
a President of the United States, while swearing to
execute the office of President of the United States,
and to the best of his ability to preserve, protect,
and defend the Constitution of the United States,
almost in the same breath declaring his adhesion and
fidelity to the doctrine of State sovereignty, a doc-

trine, or rather heresy, which the Constitution of the United States was mainly, if not explicitly, designed to obviate and eliminate from the country, and which every sound and safe statesman throughout the world regarded then, and still regards, as meaning disunion and the destruction of the Constitution and Government of the United States, and which was indeed being invoked at Jackson's time under the name of Nullification for the express purpose of destroying the government, and was only crushed out and the Constitution and government saved by the existing fact that no considerable portion of the United States had been made ready by Democratic demagogues to return to a heresy which had given their fathers floods of trouble and distress.

Here is what General Jackson said in his inaugural address on the 4th of March, 1829:

"In regard to the rights of the separate States, I hope to be animated by a proper respect for those *sovereign members* of the Union, taking care not to confound the powers they have reserved to themselves with those they have granted to the confederacy."

In his first annual message to Congress, December 8, 1829, he uses the following language:

"I cannot, therefore, too strongly or too earnestly, from my own sense of its importance, warn you against all encroachments upon the legitimate sphere of *State sovereignty*. Sustained by its healthful and vigorous influence, the Federal system can never fall."

Here, I repeat, we have a President of the United States, while under the solemn obligations of an oath taken before the whole American people, declaring in his first official words, not fidelity to the Constitution, as his oath declares, but fidelity to an anarchical principle which was then being invoked for its destruction. And here, too, we have a sample of the folly and madness to which he had been wrought up by his Democratic advisers. We also give an extract from his veto message on the Bank of the United States, all of which was written and published before State sovereignty had culminated in the South Carolina ordinance of nullification. He says:

" The Congress, the Executive, and the Court must, each for itself, be guided by its own opinion of the Constitution. Each public officer who takes an oath to support the Constitution, swears that he will support it as he understands it, and not as it is understood by others. It is as much the duty of the House of Representatives, of the Senate, and of the President, to decide upon the constitutionality of any bill or resolution which may be presented to them for passage or approval as it is of the Supreme Judges when it may be brought before them for judicial decision ; the opinion of the Judges has no more authority over Congress than the opinion of Congress has over the Judges; and, on that point, the President is independent of both. The authority of the Supreme Court must not, therefore, be permitted to control the Congress, or the Executive, when acting in their legislative capacities, but to have only such influence as the force of their reasoning may deserve."

No such folly, no such madness, no such anarchical teaching ever could have taken place under any other party name or organization than that of Democracy.

We might here give an abundance of this kind of Democratic literature, which might be called Democratic trash, were it not for the fact that just such teachings and philosophy as these prepared the party and prepared the way for the great Democratic Rebellion of 1861.

It is only necessary to here repeat, that out of the State-sovereignty heresy, taught by nearly all the Democratic papers and orators of Jackson's day, taken up and repeated by Jackson himself, the nullification of South Carolina gradually grew into formidable proportions; and according to these orators and newspapers, and the passages from Jackson's official utterances, South Carolina should have been let alone, and allowed to break up the Constitution and government at that time. But the truth is, Jackson, Democratic as he was in all his fibre and disposition, would not, or could not, brook the defiance of his own authority, and hence upon this Democratic thread hung the peace of the country at that time, which was secured through the proclamation against nullification (a synonym of State sovereignty), December 11, 1832.

Having thus briefly sketched the first attempt to enforce State sovereignty under the existing Constitution of the United States, we will return to the Democratic warfare on internal improvements, protection to home industry, and the Bank of the United States.

CHAPTER XIII.

IN discussing political questions in a free country, we should bear in mind that so great is the amount of ignorance, depravity, passion, prejudice, cupidity, avarice, and ambition for place and power, in the most highly civilized nation,—as we are taught by history,—that all the intelligence, virtue, morality, patriotism, honesty, and religious sentiments which can be mustered into service are required to enable any people to establish and uphold a free or a representative form of government; and it is known, or ought to be known to all men, that so far as these virtues and qualities are discarded or supplanted by the influence of vicious, ambitious, and dishonest men, so far, and to the same extent, free government sinks into anarchy or despotism. Probably nearly one half of mankind, in their best estate, are anarchists, or foes to good order and civil government of any kind, and hence the elements and materials with which ambitious and dishonest men deal, and out of which anarchy or despotism arise. " Organized society," says a writer of distinction, " at its best is but a thin crust over a seething ocean of evil and destructive passions, which continually threaten to break through and destroy."

94

But we must now return to a more detailed account of the reactionary and vandal programme set on foot by the great Democratic leaders soon after they found themselves in control of the government. At the time of the meeting of Congress in December, 1829, there seems to have been no party platform, or programme, marked out or agreed upon, except perhaps the dogma of State sovereignty, which was to be kept permanently before the people. This is evident from the Democratic speeches of the day, and from Jacksons own utterances previously quoted, as well as from his entire silence in his first message concerning other parts of this programme. Until Congress had met in 1829, the Democratic chiefs had no opportunity to concoct or agree upon a plan by which the great measures of the fathers were to be assailed, or as to whether they should be assailed at all. Consequently, neither Jackson nor the public knew any thing about it until after his first message had been delivered. And here it may be mentioned that the leaders, rather than the party as a whole, were the exclusive authors of this plan; for there never was a Democratic party as a whole that ever had any thing to do with the construction of a platform, unless they saw in it some terrible vengeance to be visited upon their opponents, or the destruction of some great measure or time-honored policy of the country.

It is hardly to be denied that the rank and file of a genuine Democratic party generally follow its leaders with as much precision, docility, and rapidity, as a drove of Kentucky mules driven through a city street, and with as little regard to policy, or the turns to be made, or the work to be done, provided always that the spoils of office and public plunder are kept distinctly in view. We repeat, therefore, the programme of this civil revolution and material destruction must have been concocted after the delivery of Jackson's first annual message in 1829, and the suddenness with which he, the President, was brought to its approval and acceptance constitutes one of the most astounding specimens of political jugglery and change ever witnessed among civilized men in time of peace, and such as no party or party leaders could have accomplished with their chief, outside of a Democratic party.

The Cumberland Road, which had been commenced under Jefferson's administration, from the Atlantic to the Western States, was intended to have branches to the principal cities of the West, and had already received appropriations from Congress to the amount of two million five hundred thousand dollars, besides appropriations to various other roads and canals. The leading internal-improvement measure of this Congress was for a branch of this national road from Maysville to Lexington, Kentucky, about sixty miles in length. The bill appropriating the necessary funds having passed both branches of Congress, and having been vetoed by the President, afforded the first development of the Democratic programme of reaction against the policy of the fathers. This took place on the 27th of May, 1830.

At that time appropriations by the general government were supposed to afford the only available means of opening easy and efficient intercommuni-

cation, or lines of travel and transportation for stock
and products of the soil and other merchandise, back
and forth over the Alleghany Mountains.   And, in
truth, these appropriations were, and had been for a
long time, exercising a potent influence in opening
and improving the Western country.   It is true that
the enterprise of individuals and of the State governments on the Atlantic side was spending millions of
dollars with these great ends and benefits in view.
But no such undertaking had succeeded, except the
great New York canal, an enterprise that has been
induced and stimulated by the possibility of forming
through the break in the mountain chain and in connection with the great lakes a water-line of communication with the great West.   These features and
encouragements were not presented to any other
State.   The only hope, therefore, of opening a line of
communication from any other Atlantic port to the
West was through and by means of aid from the
general government, as thirty years of struggle and
failure, even after the introduction of railroads without national aid, proved to be the case.

The Democratic party claimed in those days, as all
Democratic parties do, to contain the only friends of
the poor and laboring men; and although this national internal-improvement system was, and had
been for many years, giving employment to thousands of laboring men, and was opening new sections
of country in which they were to seek and secure
homes for themselves and families; and although the
system had received the sanction and approval of
every President and almost every other statesman

down to that time, these Democratic leaders and
would-be friends of the laboring man were at that
time concocting, and did concoct, a policy to tear
the system up by the roots, to the destruction of the
labor and enterprise of the country,—a policy which
was executed not by reason, logic, or sound statesmanship, but by exciting the passions, prejudices,
and animosities of an excitable chief magistrate, and
by the use of his veto, all of which great changes and
revolutionary measures were inaugurated and set on
foot in less than six months after Jackson had delivered his first annual message, containing the con-
gratulations, sentiments, and facts regarding the
condition of the country, its finances, and needs, as
quoted in the foregoing chapter. And thus was inaugurated that programme of Democratic vandalism
which soon plunged the country first into unparalleled
financial distress, and started it on the road to the
terrible civil war which eventually ensued. This
same party still hovers like a dark and threatening
cloud over our country, charged, doubtless, with the
same elements and means of disaster and ruin.

But here the question arises, what were the motives, what were the objects that animated this
Democratic conclave, or cabal, to put this vandal
programme into operation, and push it until the
people were precipitated over the precipice into a
gulf of ruin, darkness, and death? The answer is
plain. It all grew out of the fact, as everybody now
knows, that the internal-improvement system, the
protective tariff, and the Bank of the United States
had found their chief advocates and supporters in

Henry Clay, Daniel Webster, John M. Clayton, and other great opponents of Jackson's elevation to the Presidency, and that this Democratic cabal saw no other way to destroy their influence with the people than to lead their hoodwinked hordes, as Democratic hordes are always led by adroit chiefs, to unconsciously destroy themselves, provided that in doing so they could destroy the greatest and best men of the country; which piece of history goes far to demonstrate the utter want of patriotism, the utter want of statesmanship, and the utter want of common sense and common honesty in a great Democratic party.

The question also arises, Did these party tactics, or, more properly speaking, did this party trickery have the effect of putting a stop to appropriations for internal improvements? For a short time it did; but it had a still greater effect in destroying the honesty and patriotic motives upon which such appropriations had been made. In their stead there grew up a system of bargaining, a system of "log-rolling" appropriations, which soon grew into vastly augmented proportions, in which Democratic politicians have always been conspicuous as shareholders.

Whether it was the ambition of the Democratic leaders to overreach and overthrow their opponents, regardless of the best interests of the country; whether from the natural and instinctive depravity of such a party; or whether from a providential blindness brought upon the people that they might be punished for some cherished sin, the veto of the Maysville Road bill was the beginning and the first step in a downward policy, which deprived the Southern States of their rightful share of national appropriations, thus consigning them to comparative poverty and weakness for the next thirty years, and finally ending in the entire prostration of business throughout the country, as such tactics always do end with any people, where the party is in the ascendant long enough to accomplish such a result.

It should be also observed that this act fell upon the country like a clap of thunder in a clear sky. It gave a fearful shock to business, it dazed politicians, put a stop to many enterprises and threw thousands of laboring men out of employment; and before the country had recovered, other parts of this terrible programme came into effect, and so the people were driven or dragged into terrible demoralization and disasters by the party in power.

CHAPTER XIV.

THE PROTECTIVE TARIFF AND DEMOCRATIC WARFARE AGAINST IT.—HENRY CLAY.

IT is a well-known fact that the most able advocates of a protective tariff were first found in the Southern States, and that, under their support and encouragement, manufacturing establishments, both North and South, had their first rapid and substantial growth. It is true that, owing to the sterility of the soil and the frigidity of the climate along the Northern coast, the Northern establishments had their most rapid growth, and that owing to the profitableness of the culture of cotton, rice, tobacco, and sugar, which were then assuming large proportions in the South, the manufacturing establishments there were not so numerous or large as at the North. But it is nevertheless true, that there arose in the South, under such a tariff, many cotton, iron, and other mechanical establishments which proved to be highly profitable. These were found in great numbers, for those times, in Maryland, Virginia, North Carolina, and Georgia. Nor have the Southern States or the entire country ever been more prosperous and thriving, at any time, than under the highest tariffs yet levied up to the present day. And though the Northern States took the lead in manufacturing enterprises, it may be said, considering the fascinations of cotton-planting and other Southern interests, such as rice, tobacco, sugar, and lumber, that there was no reasonable ground for the South to complain, or be dissatisfied with a protective tariff, as a candid and careful review of the situation, during those years, will clearly demonstrate to the understanding of all honest and truth-loving men.

But no sooner had Democracy begun to show itself, and Democratic clubs and Democratic organizations begun to be formed from 1820 to 1824, than the Democratic spirit, true to its instincts and traditions, began to seek for men and measures to be attacked, and some great policy to be overturned, or rather its leaders began to assail the protective tariff, and many of them went so far as to oppose the tariff, as a means of obtaining any revenue, with a vigor and ferocity that would have done credit to hungry wolves dashing upon a flock of sheep, and such as none but such leaders ever manifest. The first premeditated and combined attack upon this policy was made in 1824, when Gen. Jackson was first brought forward as the first Democratic candidate for the Presidency. Nor were such attacks confined to the Democratic leaders of the South. Pennsylvania and New York, and especially the city of New York, the hottest hot-bed of Democracy and Democratic ferocity on the American continent,— the city of New York, the great emporium, or the great inlet and outlet through which nearly all our foreign trade is carried on, and by means of which astute merchants, operators, and speculators, who were of course advocates of free trade, such as would close every manufacturing shop in America, are enabled to gather into their coffers the chief wealth of the country,—joined hand-in-hand with Southern Democrats in this wild and anti-American crusade against a protective tariff. And hence we must repeat that the astute merchants, operators, and speculators in that hottest and most dangerous hot-bed of Democracy in the world, very well understood that if American manufactories could be kept down, as they would be, under a free-trade policy, all or nearly all the vast imports and supplies for this country, and all or nearly all the vast products of the country for sale, would have to pass through New York, thereby collecting all or nearly all the wealth of the country into that great city; and hence it is, too, these astute leaders availed themselves of the hordes of ignorant Europeans who flock to that city to fill up the ranks of free-trade Democracy, and thereby strengthen a policy whose chief influence and end was to rob and plunder honest, industrious, and enterprising Americans of the fruits of their labor. It was this most corrupt and untrustworthy body of politicians ever known, that caressed and shouted "bravo" to the Southern Nullifiers, when they were trying to push the constitution and government of the United States to the wall, because of the protective policy. Nor should it be forgotten that this school of politicians is at the present time flooding the country with free-trade tracts, from their free-trade league, that they may thus further gorge themselves with the legitimate and rightful products of the honest industry and enterprise of the country at large.

There seem to be two schools of writers on political economy in this country. One contends for free trade, or the abolition of all tariffs; and the other, that there is no science or universal rule in political economy: and as these conflicting views gave much trouble to the Jacksonian Democracy, and still agitate men's minds, it may not be out of place to touch upon the subject, so far as to say:

First, that it is the duty of every civil government to encourage and protect the commercial and industrial interests of its own people, as against the arts and management of rival governments.

Second, that every nation of people has interests peculiar to itself, to be encouraged, guarded, and protected by its government and by suitable legislation.

Third, the best, if not the only, method of protection known to commercial nations in time of peace, is by a tariff, or impost, upon importations of such articles as come into competition with home products.

Fourth, that such a tax is divided between the producers and consumers, the foreign producer paying about one half, thus lightening to that extent the burdens on the consumer.

It is acknowledged, at least by most people, that these are self-evident truths in political economy, and therefore worthy the consideration of statesmen. But as it is not so much the object of these pages to analyze theories as to give historical facts which illustrate Democratic proclivities, we must go on with the narration. As heretofore observed, no sooner had this party come into possession of supreme power, whether from natural instinct or deliberate design, every great measure of the fathers was assailed with great bitterness, the leaders adopting the motto that to the victors belong the spoils, thus trampling upon every principle of free government and equal rights, counted sound and safe by the fathers.

These assaults were made, some from one point and some from another, some from one motive and some from another, according to the locality and interest of the attacking parties, and the prospect and hope of reward. Among the prominent suggestions was a scheme for the application of the dogma of State sovereignty, under the name and style of " nullification,"—namely, the right of a State to abrogate a tariff levied by the government of the United States upon imports. This, we repeat, was one of the ways in which Democracy claimed the right to act as it pleases, just as soon as a majority of the people of the State could be brought up to the point of resistance. To make out a case that was adequate to fire up the people, this branch of the Democracy, which had its headquarters in South Carolina, put forth what was called in those days " the forty-bale theory." It may be stated in this way. South Carolina claimed to raise and export eight million dollars' worth of cotton per annum. The tariff was estimated to be forty per cent. on the cost of articles imported under it. Of course, coffee, tea, and some other imported

articles paid little or no duty. Yet the South Carolina Democrats claimed that out of each one hundred
bales of cotton, forty bales were required to pay the
tariff duties on imported goods consumed in that
State. Or, in other words, that forty hundredths of
the eight million dollars' worth of cotton raised in
the State, or two million six hundred thousand dollars, was consumed in paying the duties on the imported goods consumed in the State. This the
Democratic leaders made their Democratic followers
believe was the truth, notwithstanding that Henry
Clay, the great patriot of his day, demonstrated to
them on the floor of Congress, that instead of two
million six hundred thousand dollars paid by the
people of South Carolina on account of the tariff,
they paid less than three hundred and fifty thousand
dollars, or about one tenth of the amount claimed
to be paid. But, notwithstanding all this, the Democrats, having a majority in the State, drove ahead,
and passed an ordinance to nullify the tariff in South
Carolina, the Constitution and Government of the
United States to the contrary notwithstanding.

This case affords a fair example of Democratic
reasoning, or rather its recklessness and disregard of
reason, when it cannot have its own way. Or, to
present this piece of history in other language,
Democracy, with the theory of State sovereignty as
a sweet morsel under its tongue, in the name and
style of nullification, actually set on foot in 1832,
without rhyme or reason, an insurrection which
boded fearful calamities to our country, but which
fortunately was nipped in the bud, because neither

the American people, nor the Southern people had been sufficiently contaminated by Democratic sentiments to allow it to spread, and because General Jackson, with all his faults, was too much of a patriot to stand by and see the Constitution and flag of his country torn into shreds by a Democratic faction; and hence the proclamation of Jackson, which struck nullification between the eyes. It was written by the great " Defender of the Constitution," Daniel Webster, and acted like oil upon troubled water, until another Democratic insurrection was set on foot.

But as this nullification movement occupied quite a large space in the history of the country, and comprised the beginning of those Democratic tactics which led to the great Rebellion, and inasmuch as the circumstances and relations in connection with the tariff are nearly the same now in 1883 as they were in 1832, the reader will not object to some extracts from Mr. Clay, covering the main grounds of the controversy, and meeting the same kind of arguments made by free-trade advocates at the present time. He spoke as follows in February, 1832:

"But it is confidently argued that the import duty falls upon the growth of cotton; and the case has been put in debate, and again and again in conversation, of the South Carolina planter who exports one hundred bales of cotton to Liverpool, exchanges them for one hundred bales of merchandise, and when he brings them home, is compelled to leave at the custom-house forty bales in the form of duties. The argument is founded on

the assumption that a duty of forty per centum
amounts to a subtraction of forty from the one hundred bales of merchandise. The first objection to
it is, that it supposes a case of barter which never
occurs. If it be replied, that it nevertheless occurs
in the operations of commerce, the answer would be,
that since the export of Carolina cotton is chiefly
made by New York or foreign merchants, the loss
stated, if it really accrued, would fall upon them,
and not upon the planter. But to test the correctness of the hypothetical case, let us suppose that
the duty, instead of forty per centum, should be one
hundred and fifty, which is asserted to be the duty
in some cases. Then the planter would not only
lose the whole hundred bales of merchandise—merchandise which he had gotten for his hundred bales
of cotton, but he would have to purchase, with other
means, an additional fifty bales, in order to enable him
to pay the duties accruing on the proceeds of the
cotton. Another answer is, that if the *producer* of
cotton in America, exchanged against English fabrics,
pays the duty, the *producer* of those fabrics also pays
it, and then it is twice paid. Such must be the consequence, unless the principle is true on the one side
of the Atlantic, and false on the other. The true
answer is, that the exporter of an article, if he
invests its proceeds in a foreign market, takes care to
make the investment in such merchandise as, when
brought home, he can sell with a fair profit; and,
consequently, the consumer would pay the original
cost and charges and profit."

"The next objection to the American system is

that it subjects South Carolina to the payment of
an undue proportion of the public revenue. The
basis of this objection is the assumption, shown to
have been erroneous, that the producer of the exports from this country pays the duty on its imports,
instead of the consumer of those imports. No
more than that of any other States, can the amount
which South Carolina really contributes to the
public revenue be precisely ascertained. It depends
upon her consumption of articles paying duties, and
we may make an approximation sufficient for all
practical purposes. The cotton planters of the valley
of the Mississippi with whom I am acquainted, generally expend about one third of their income in the
support of their families and plantations. On this
subject I hold in my hands a statement from a
friend of mine, of great accuracy, and a member of
the Senate. According to this statement, in a crop
of ten thousand dollars, the expenses may fluctuate
between two thousand eight hundred dollars and
three thousand two hundred dollars. Of this sum,
about one fourth, from seven to eight hundred
dollars, may be laid out in articles paying the protective duty; the residue is disbursed for provision,
mules, horses, oxen, wages of overseer, etc. Esti-
mating the exports of South Carolina at eight
millions, one third is two millions six hundred and
sixty-six thousand six hundred and sixty-six dollars;
of which one fourth will be six hundred and sixty-
six thousand six hundred and sixty-six and two-
thirds dollars. Now, supposing the protection to be
fifty per centum, and that it all enters into the price of

the article, the amount paid by South Carolina would only be three hundred and thirty-three thousand three hundred and thirty-three and one third dollars. But the total revenue of the United States may be stated at twenty-five millions, of which the proportion of South Carolina, whatever standard, whether of wealth or population, be adopted, would be about one million. Of course, on this view of the subject, she actually pays only about one third of her fair and legitimate share."

Such was the analysis of the " forty-bale theory " of South Carolina, by the greatest statesman of his age, but which would never, owing to its absurdity, have been seriously discussed by Mr. Clay, had not that State been placed in a false position, and flattered with false hopes by Democratic leaders in all other parts of the country, and had it not been for the unmitigated calumny and abuse heaped by them upon the great statesmen, and the great measures which had brought the country to the prosperous condition spoken of by Jackson in 1829. But let us see how the protective tariff, against which Democracy was everywhere arrayed, operated upon the interests of the country in those days. To do this we must give a few more extracts from the same speech of the same great patriot.

" But it is contended, in the last place, that the South cannot, from physical and other causes, engage in the manufacturing arts. I deny the premises, and I deny the conclusion ; I deny the fact of inability ; and if it existed, I deny the conclusion, that we must, therefore, break down our manufactures, and nourish those of foreign countries. The South possesses, in an extraordinary degree, two of the most important elements of manufacturing industry, water-power and labor. The former gives to our whole country a most decided advantage over Great Britain."

He also says, of the benefits of a high tariff:

" I plant myself upon this fact, of cheapness and superiority, as upon impregnable ground. Gentlemen may tax their ingenuity, and produce a thousand speculative solutions of the fact, but the fact itself will remain undisturbed. Let us look into some particulars. The total consumption of bar-iron in the United States is supposed to be about one hundred and forty-six thousand tons, of which one hundred and twelve thousand eight hundred and sixty-six tons are made within the country, and the residue imported. The number of men employed in the manufacture is estimated at twenty-nine thousand two hundred and fifty-four, and the total number of persons subsisted by it, at one hundred and forty-six thousand two hundred and seventy-three. The measure of protection extended to this necessary article was never fully adequate until the passage of the act of 1828; and what has been the consequence? The annual increase of quantity, since that period, has been in a ratio of near twenty-five per centum, and the wholesale price of bar-iron in the Northern cities was, in 1828, one hundred and five dollars per ton ; in 1829, one hundred dollars ; in 1830, ninety dollars ; and in 1831, from eighty-five to seventy-five dollars, constantly diminishing.

*　　*　　*　　*　　*　　*

" My honorable friend from Massachusetts, now in my eye (Mr. Silsbee), informed me, that on his departure from home, among the last orders which he gave, one was for the exportation of coarse cotton to Sumatra, in the vicinity of Calcutta. I hold in my hand a statement derived from the most authentic source, showing that the identical description of cotton cloth, which sold in 1817 at twenty-nine cents per yard, was sold in 1819 at twenty-one cents, in 1821 at nineteen and a half cents, in 1823 at seventeen cents, in 1825 at fourteen and a half cents, in 1827 at thirteen cents, in 1828 at nine cents, in 1830 at nine and a half cents, and in 1831 at from ten and a half to eleven. Such is the wonderful effect of protection, competition, and improvement in skill, combined!"

Now, whether we make deductions from the history and operations of a tariff as a means of revenue and protection, or whether we draw conclusions from these words of Mr. Clay, or from hundreds of other facts and arguments put forth in those days by other old Whigs, we must acknowledge:

First, that a protective tariff, that is to say, a tariff for revenue, with discriminations in favor of home industry, was highly beneficial to the entire country, North and South, inasmuch as Gen. Jackson and Mr. Clay agreed in affirming that the country had never before been in so prosperous a condition.

Second, that opposition to the tariff and nullification sprung from the State-sovereignty dogma, and the force and influence given to both, the one and the other, by Democratic organs and orators in all parts of the country.

Third, that it was the danger and influence thus imparted to them by Democratic leaders, together with the dread and fear of civil strife and bloodshed in our country, that induced the old Whigs, with Mr. Clay at their head, to abandon the protective system, in the adoption of the so-called Clay Compromise of 1833.

Fourth, that the abandonment of the protective system was one of the great causes that contributed to the fearful financial and material crash of 1837.

And fifth, that the vandal and destructive policy of the Democracy struck the country when it was more prosperous, both North and South, than it had ever been before, and that in about seven years this policy reduced the country to a depth of misery and distress never before seen or suffered by any country in a time of peace.

CHAPTER XV.

THE main study, the main policy, and the chief ambition of the Democratic leaders in Jackson's day was to destroy the Bank of the United States. To this end Democratic newspapers, Democratic discourses in and out of Congress, in and out of office, were larded and interlarded with anti-bank literature, anti-bank logic, and anti-bank sophistry. And besides these, many Presidential messages and many official reports were wholly framed and directed to convince the people of the United States that they had no need of a national bank, and no need of a national paper currency to carry on their minute or their vast industries and commerce, and that such institutions were dangerous to liberty, and solely designed to rob them of their property and their just rights. For ten long years, extending through Jackson's and Van Buren's administrations, this anti-bank literature and anti-bank sophistry loaded the Democratic presses, and burdened the mails of the country, to the exclusion of almost everything that was patriotic and useful to the people. And as experience has since demonstrated, this was a clear case in which the folly and madness of men in authority were allowed by the providence of God to prevail over wisdom and sound statesmanship, that He, the Ruler of nations, might punish the people, or that they might punish themselves, for some great national sin. In this, as in most other cases, when a Democratic party comes to the front, the Democracy became the scourge of the people, as the Philistines became a scourge to the ancient Israelites, on account of their sins. And here we must leave it to the Democracy of to-day to say whether the relation their fathers occupied to the country on that occasion is an honor or a disgrace to their party at this time.

And yet so great was the interest the people had and felt in a national currency, in a national bank with its twenty-five branches, notwithstanding the tons and thousands of tons of anti-bank literature and sophistry foisted upon them for ten or twelve years by these mad and ambitious statesmen, in 1840, the people placed their seal of condemnation on all the conclusions of this literary and political trash, by the election of a bank congress and William Henry Harrison to the Presidency. And yet again, for some inscrutable purpose, God, in his providence, through the early death of Harrison, changed this victory of the people to ashes upon their lips, and the national currency and the bank went by the board for the time being, accompanied by calamities upon the people, beyond the power of man to estimate or describe. But let us inquire for a few moments what it was that this party of ambitious madmen destroyed, in destroying these institutions.

It is well known that when modern nations began

to rise from the dark ages, and engage in commerce and manufactures, they also began to use, as a medium for the transfer of values, bills of exchange, and other paper representatives of money. Such mediums may have been suggested at first by the scarcity of the precious metals, and the greater convenience and safety of carriage. These bits of paper representing money were doubtless first issued by wealthy merchants of high moral standing. But out of this practice soon grew frauds and failures to redeem these bits of paper according to promise. So convenient, however, was this paper medium found to be in the various forms and transactions of trade, that even with these frauds and failures, the people of civilized communities continued to use it, rather than to be burdened with, and suffer the dangers incident to, metallic money. And in fact it was also ascertained that much trade could be carried on by means of this paper medium, which could not be safely conducted without it. And hence it was not long before commercial men began to call for the establishment of what were called banks, under the guaranty of the government, and for the quadruple purpose of obtaining a safe paper currency, a safe place of deposit both for the people and the government, safe bills of exchange both for the people and the government, and institutions from which both the people and the government could borrow money in cases of need ; and which they found to be of great convenience and value, both to the people and the government in their thousands of financial transactions. These, we repeat, were the chief reasons, and sufficient reasons, why banks and paper-money were brought into existence.

From this state of things, and from the nature of trade and finance, we naturally infer came national banks—that is to say, banks in which the government took a part of the stock and a leading part in the management, and especially a leading part in the redemption or guaranty of this paper representation of money ; the government itself being rewarded for its service by getting thereby a safe place of deposit for its funds, cheap and safe exchange, and loans at low rate of interest, but above all, a safe paper currency for the people, which objects were, and should be, as a matter of course, of paramount importance with any government worthy the name of government.

It is out of trade, commerce, and manufactures among the people, that all governments of civilized people derive their support, which important truth, by the way, seems never to have found a lodgment in the heads of Democratic leaders or Democratic statesmen, during all the times in which they have had the control of the government of this country. In no other way can we account for the warfare the party has always made upon trade, commerce, and manufactures combined, and, through these great features of modern civilization, war upon the great interests of agriculture, and of the people in general.

Banks had been in general use in European countries more than two hundred years before the government of the United States came into existence. The national bank of Venice had been in operation about six hundred years, and had probably been the chief source of the great prosperity and strength of that republic during several hundred years. All this our forefathers well understood, and having witnessed frequent failures of local banks and their utter inadequacy to supply the proper currency, suitable exchanges, and safe places of deposit for successful commerce, one of their first great acts under our present Constitution was to charter a Bank of the United States, which was done in 1791.

It is true, that at the time many good men opposed the measure, upon the ground of supposed unconstitutionality, and because they counted it an offspring and instrument of monarchy. But so great and so numerous were the advantages, and so great was the increase of wealth in those nations which had adopted a national bank, over those nations which had not, and so great was the need in our country of such an institution, that Washington himself and a large majority of the Congress gave it their support, the government itself subscribing for a part of the stock. It ran its course of twenty years, and proved to be of signal benefit to the government and the people. But its charter having expired in 1811, owing to the prevalence at that time of what was called Jeffersonian Democracy, and some scruples in the mind of President Madison as to its constitutionality, it failed at that time to obtain a renewal of its charter. The war with Great Britain came on in 1812, and the country and the government itself were soon plunged into a most deplorable and pitiable condition. State banks failed, money and credit—both private and public—

disappeared, and it was with the utmost difficulty
that the government and the people contended with
the few thousand soldiers that England was able to
send over at that time. For the want of funds, both
private and public, many parts of the country were
ravaged, our maritime commerce was destroyed, and
the city of Washington itself was captured by a
British army so small that American patriots have
felt a tinge of shame from that day to this.

But the war being over, the same Jeffersonian
Democrats, as they still call themselves, having seen
the terrible ravages and suffering of the government
and the people for the want of such an institution,
in a fit of patriotism, brought upon them by hard
licks, assisted in chartering another bank of the
United States. This took place in 1816, President
Madison, himself, giving the charter his approval.

It was under the influence and financial assistance
of this bank, that the government and people of the
United States reached the pitch of prosperity and
happiness already set forth in these pages, and
which are very well remembered by many living
men. But, in an evil hour, in the cloisters of darkness, or the caucuses of the newly formed Jackson
Democracy, the institution was marked for destruction. This bank, according to the suggestions of
Jackson, in 1829, was re-chartered, so far as Congress
could do it, by a large majority in each House, but
the bill was vetoed by Jackson, July 10, 1832. If we
have not already made clear that none but a Democratic party and a Democratic President could have
been embarked in so crazy, so cruel, and so disas-

trous a crusade against the interest of the government and the people, we trust it will be clear to the
understanding of every reader, when we shall have
reviewed the terrible condition into which, in the
course of a few years thereafter, the country was
plunged by this Democratic crusade.

CHAPTER XVI.

THOMAS H. BENTON was the veritable father of the present Democratic party. All sects and parties have a leader or a chief who may be styled its father. Benton was the great stumper of the campaign in which Jackson was first elected to the Presidency. During the early stages of this party many of Jackson's friends called it the Jackson party. Many of them were strongly inclined to hold to the word Republican as a party name, but Benton insisted on its being called the Democratic party, and his voice prevailed, thus entitling him to the appellation of "father." But he is entitled to be called its father from other points of view. According to his own account and well remembered facts, he was the champion and animating spirit in the warfare against the measures and policy of the fathers, sought to be overthrown by this party ; perhaps we should say more especially in the warfare against the Bank of the United States, upon the destruction of which the party staked its entire hopes and fortunes. Indeed, he was the chief debater and boss of the party for twenty years, beginning with Jackson's first administration and ending with that of James K. Polk, when the party spewed him out, as all Democratic parties do with a leader when it finds he can no longer control and direct the spoils of office and public plunder.

It is well known that Benton was a man of great industry and varied talents, but it would be an omission not to observe that he was the most egotistical, vain, and pompous character ever produced by this or any other country, and was in every way fitted to be a successful Democratic leader. He was impudent, dictatorial, and arrogant in his manners. And if we should say he was more reckless, audacious, and unscrupulous, and dealt more in political promises, predictions, and prophecies that time proved to be illusory, false, and pernicious than any other man of his generation, we should not vary far from the truth. Nor can any one prove that he was not the veritable father of modern Democracy and responsible for the nefarious tactics and principles the party put in operation as soon as it got possession of supreme power.

Benton was a sort of modern Alcibiades, without his military qualities, or perhaps it would be more appropriate to say he was a modern Mirabeau, a Danton, or a Robespierre, without the opportunity of putting into execution their bloody programmes. He was both reactionary and revolutionary, suggesting and upholding practices and measures which, if carried out, would always call for the bottom rails of society to be placed on top, or, more properly speaking, would produce a despotism based upon and supported by the lowest strata of society, as was the case under his prototypes in France during her memorable Revolution. His faculty for calumny and

detraction, or, to speak in plain Saxon, his faculty
for adroit blackguardism and his power of blackening
great characters and sound political principles
were unsurpassed by his French prototypes, and
under the same circumstances and among the same
kind of people, must have led to the same results as
theirs did. If he had any settled plan of statesmanship, it must have been the division of the Union
into three parts, the North, the South, and the
West, over the last of which he hoped to be boss
for life. Certain it is, no man had ever lived since
the Declaration of Independence who did so much
to alienate the three sections of the country. The
audacity, arrogance, and fiendish disposition of the
man are manifest by his often-repeated assertion that
the excitement and distress of the people were all
" about nothing."

But it must be confessed, however, that the advent
of a Democratic party to power, when the country
was prosperous and at peace with all the world, was
favorable to the operations of such a party, and such
a boss as Benton, and the consequent ravages that
followed, inasmuch as there was but little room for
improvement on the policy and measures pursued
and adopted by the patriots who had ruled the
country for the previous twenty years, and inasmuch
as a Democratic party, if not revolutionary and
destructive of what has been built up, is not in its
true element, nor performing its natural and instinctive mission.

It is well remembered by all old men that Benton's
numerous speeches were distributed by tons and

hundreds of tons throughout the country by his admirers and by the Democratic administration. Every
house was reached by them, and his most extravagant and vile assertions were swallowed and followed
by the rank and file of the party with a gusto and
shouts that would have done honor to a Parisian
Democratic mob in the heyday of Jacobinism.
But fortunately for our country and the world,
and as had been done with some of the men to
whom we have compared him, public sentiment
spewed him out of all places of honor and power,
and his days were ended before the great conflict,
which his course and conduct helped to inaugu-
rate, began. The chief and last effort of his
ambition was to get himself appointed by President Polk commander-in-chief of the army in Mexico,
which had just achieved the conquest of that country under Generals Taylor and Scott, who were, notwithstanding their brilliant military achievements,
to be punished for being old Whigs, while Democracy was to be exalted in the person of Benton.
Pending the confirmation by the Senate, which, by
the way, was never obtained, Benton strutted up
and down the streets of Washington in his "regi-
mentals," like a certain bird distinguished for the
length and brilliancy of its feathers. Such, we repeat, was the chief boss and 'father of the present
Democratic party, and as this modern Hercules
claimed to be the slayer of the bank, as he unquestionably was the chief enemy of the long-cherished
interests of the people, he is commended to the
tender care of the party which he had done so much

to organize, and had successfully bossed for twenty years.

Benton made, in 1831, the first speech in Congress against the recharter of the bank. It occupied nearly a week in its delivery, and the following are extracts from the same, with his account of it, found in his " Thirty Years in the United States Senate." He says :

" From the time of President Jackson's intimations against the recharter of the bank " (?) " in the annual message of 1829, there had been a ceaseless and prevailing activity in behalf of the bank in all parts of the Union, and in all forms—in newspapers, in the halls of Congress, in the State Legislatures, even in much of the periodical literature, in the elections, and in conciliation of presses and individuals,—all conducted in a way to operate most strongly upon the public mind, and to conclude the question in the forum of the people, before it was brought forward in the National Legislature."—Vol. I, page 187.

But before commenting on this passage, in order to show the defectiveness of memory, not to say the self-contradiction of this verbose and loud-mouthed boaster, and his untrustworthiness, we here give what he said in commenting on the bank veto, which took place the year after this speech was delivered. He says:

" The appearance of the veto message was the signal for the delivery of the great speeches of the advocates of the bank. Thus far they had held back, refraining from general debate, and limiting themselves to brief answers to current objections.

Now they came forth in all their strength, in speeches elaborate and studied, and covering the whole ground of constitutionality and expediency, and delivered with unusual warmth and vehemence."—Vol. 1, page 254.

In reference to this first extract, the reader can hardly fail to discover the art and adroitness with which he labors to attribute the deep interest the people had and felt in the bank and its twenty-five branches, to venal selfishness of the stockholders and the statesmen who favored its recharter. In reference to the second extract, in his efforts to justify Jackson for the veto, he virtually denies all this, in order to make it appear that the veto message contained revelations concerning the interests of the people, about which they were ignorant or indifferent. But the truth is, this misrepresentation and utter perversion of the public sentiment and interest concerning the bank, by Benton and the veto message itself, together with the glorification of himself and Jackson, seems to have been the chief incentive to fully one half of his speeches, and the writing and compilation of his ponderous volumes, entitled "Thirty Years in the Senate of the United States." The comprehensive truth of the whole matter is this: The newly formed Democratic party was mainly made up of a few ambitious politicians and the most ignorant and depraved portions of society, who cared but little or nothing about the bank of the United States, or any other great leading measure, but having found, as they supposed, in Gen. Jackson a great warrior and patriot, and in Benton an apt and congenial boss for such a party, if he had said to them that the glorious old hero, as he called Jackson, was sent to overturn the Constitution of the United States from beginning to end, the whole party, or the whole power of the party, could have been launched against that sacred instrument, as in fact it was, as we shall see before we close this history. For there never was any thing too venerable or sacred for such a party to attack, or too absurd and monstrous for a Democratic party to undertake.

Benton continues his remarks on his speech thus:

"The current was all setting one way. I determined to raise a voice against it in the Senate, and made several efforts before I succeeded—the thick array of bank friends throwing every obstacle in my way, and even friends holding me back for the regular course, which was to wait, for the application for the renewed charter to be presented, and then to oppose it."

Here we perceive the pompous vanity and egotism with which he labors to install himself as the boss and hero of the wreck and ruin he so largely shared in producing.

"In the session of 1830–31," he says, "I succeeded in creating the first opportunity of delivering a speech against it; it was done a little irregularly, by submitting a negative resolution against the renewal of the charter, and taking the opportunity, while asking leave to introduce the resolution, to speak fully against the charter."

And thus was commenced the vandal warfare

against a national bank and a national currency. Here are also some extracts from his speech above referred to, as given by himself.

" I am willing to see the charter expire, without providing any substitute for the present bank. I am willing to see the currency of the Federal Government left to the hard money mentioned and· intended in the Constitution."

*   *   *   *   *   *

" The United States possess gold mines, now yielding half a million per annum, with every prospect of equalling those of Peru. But this is not the best dependence. We have what is superior to mines, namely, the exports which command the money of the world ; that is to say, the food which sustains life, and the raw materials which sustain manufactures. Gold and silver is the best currency for a republic; it suits the men of middle property and the working people best ; and if I was going to establish a workingman's party, it should be on the basis of hard money ; a hard-money party, against a paper party."

In these extracts we have specimens of the reactionary and retrograde schedule which was to be run by the Democratic leaders in reference to the policy of a national bank and a national currency, such as had long been used by the leading nations of Europe and our government, and which above all other means had fostered and extended every branch of industry and commerce, and to which reactionary and retrograde schedule almost the entire power of the Democratic party, and the

government itself, was devoted for the space of ten
or twelve years. This warfare resulted in the overthrow of almost the entire system of American
industry and commerce, thereby throwing from our
country hundreds of millions of wealth, and landing
the same in the laps of those nations which had
adopted and retained these great means of wealth
and prosperity, to say nothing here of the poverty
and distress produced by the schedule in all parts of
our country, as a matter of course.

At the time Benton was discussing the recharter
of our bank, the recharter of the Bank of England
was under consideration, and by some hocus-pocus
sagacity, which Benton always exhibited in his propensity for prophecies, he made up his own speech,
as he himself tells us, mainly from the anti-bank
speeches being made in England at that time. We
only have space for a short extract, as a sample both
of his prophetic visions and the balderdash style of
his oratory.

" Shall English lords and ladies continue to find in
the Bank of the United States, the unjust and odious
privileges which they can no longer find in the Bank
of England? Shall the copy survive here, after the
original has been destroyed there? Shall the young
whelp triumph in America, after the old lion has
been throttled and strangled in England? No!
Never! The thing is impossible! The Bank of the
United States dies, and the Bank of England dies,
in all its odious points, upon the limitation of its
charter, and the only circumstance of regret is that
the generous deliverance is to take effect two years

earlier in the British monarchy than in the American republic."

The reader need hardly be informed that the Bank of England was rechartered at that time with all its powers and privileges intact, Benton to the contrary notwithstanding, and remains to this day as the financial centre of the world, and the citadel of the glory and power of Great Britain, while the North American continent was robbed of hundreds of millions of wealth, which would have remained with us had it not been for this false prophet, this boss, and the reactionary and retrograde schedule of the Democratic party, in destroying the bank and the national currency of the United States.

CHAPTER XVII.

IT was known, or should have been known, to the Democratic leaders of Jackson's day, that there is but one way to destroy the power and influence of wealth in government, and its danger to civil liberty, and that is to destroy wealth itself, and finally reduce the community thereby to the barbaric state. On the other hand, the creation and protection of property, and the rights of property in the hands of all the citizens, go hand-in-hand with the protection and perpetuation of free government and civil liberty. It was known, or should have been known, to the Democratic leaders, that a national bank was a moral and legitimate institution,—an institution intimately connected with the industry and commerce of the country, which could only prosper as they prospered, and must fail if they fail,—an institution also designed for a safe place of deposit, and to afford bills of exchange or the transfer of funds, both for the people and the government ; all of which accommodations were, and are still, necessary for active industry and traffic of every kind. And inasmuch as such a bank or banks have always been divided in their management and control between the government and the citizens ; and inasmuch as the stock or property in the bank has generally been divided into shares so small that each property-holder may have an ownership therein; and inasmuch as it is and must be the interest of the bank, in promoting its own interest, to promote the interest and prosperity of the people, it cannot be antagonistic to civil government and civil liberty. But all these considerations were counted as nothing by the Democratic leaders; and their entire anti-bank literature, amounting to thousands of tons, prating and forever prating about monopolies for the space of ten or a dozen years, was stamped and condemned by the world as mere hypocritical cant, when these same leaders set themselves to work to create out of the Treasury of the United States, and did create, a bank a thousand times more powerful and dangerous, in the management of which the citizens had, and could have, no direct influence or control.

The chief influence and popularity of the Democratic party in those days arose from the fact that Gen. Jackson had been commander at the time, and had won the battle of New Orleans in 1814, which, as De Tocqueville thought, formed a very slight foundation for a President of the United States. As it was, he became, as it were, by virtue of this victory and his reckless audacity, or rather by his obedience to his confidential advisers, the Allah of his party, and Benton its prophet. As a general rule, their followers knew and cared as little about the Bank of the United States, as they did about the House of Stuart, or the Orleans branch of the Bourbons, nor did they perceive the inevitable destruction of the business and industries its overthrow would produce. They

cared no more for the advice and statesmanship of
such men as Alexander Hamilton, Albert Gallatin,
Henry Clay, and Daniel Webster, than they cared
for the introduction of Christianity among the nations
of the East. And hence it was that the party followed its leaders in their reckless ambition to overthrow the bank, and in doing so, to turn down such
men as Clay, Webster, and Clayton, until the whole
country was involved in a catastrophe, which came
near being as disastrous to the American people as
was the destruction of Jerusalem by the Romans to
the ancient Jews. And here we have another glimpse,
or a clear insight, into the ever-present danger of
the despotism and wreck and ruin flowing from the
existence and unchecked control of a Democratic
party in possession of supreme power.

I Iaving now given, in our own words, some account
of the course and policy of the Democratic leaders,
it becomes altogether proper to give the reader
some contemporary expressions and statements from
the great statesmen of that day who favored the
bank and other policies of the fathers.

After Benton had thrust his long and arrogant
speech upon the Senate against the bank, and after
his party and the government itself had printed and
circulated millions of copies, the Republican, *alias*
the Whig, party held a convention in Baltimore, December, 1831, in which as a part of their proceedings
and platform they put forth the following presentation of the subject:

· "Next to the great measures of policy which protect and encourage domestic industry, the most im-

portant question connected with the economical policy of the country is that of the bank. This great and beneficial institution, by facilitating exchanges between different parts of the Union and maintaining a sound, ample, and healthy state of the currency, may be said to supply the body politic, economically viewed, with a continual stream of life-blood, without which it must inevitably languish and sink into exhaustion. It was first conceived and organized by the powerful mind of Hamilton. After having been temporarily shaken by the honest though groundless scruples of other statesmen, it has been recalled to existence by the general consent of all parties, and with the universal approbation of the people. Under the ablest and most faithful management it has been for many years past pursuing a course of steady and constantly increasing influence. Such is the institution which the President has gone out of his way, in several successive messages, without a pretence of necessity, or plausible motive in the first instance, six years before his suggestion could with any propriety be acted upon, to denounce to Congress as a sort of nuisance, and to consign, as far as his influence extends, to immediate destruction.

"For this denunciation no pretext of any adequate motive is assigned. At a time when the institution is known to all to be in the most efficient and prosperous state,—to be doing all that any bank ever did or can do,—we are briefly told in ten words, that it has not effected the objects for which it was instituted, and must be abolished. Another institution is recommended as a substitute, which, so far as the description given of it can be understood, would be no better than a machine in the hands of the government for fabricating and issuing paper-money without check or responsibility. In his recent message to Congress the President declares, for the third time, his opinion on these subjects in the same concise and authoritative style as before, and intimates that he shall consider his re-election as an expression of the opinion of the people that they ought to be acted upon. If, therefore, the President be re-elected, it may be considered certain that the bank will be abolished, and the institution which he has recommended, or something like it, substituted in its place.

"Are the people of the United States prepared for this? Are they ready to destroy one of their most valuable establishments to gratify the caprice of a chief magistrate, who reasons and advises upon a subject with the details of which he is evidently unacquainted, in direct contradiction to the opinion of his own official consellors? Are the enterprising, liberal, high-minded, and intelligent merchants of the Union willing to countenance such a measure? Are the cultivators of the West, who find in the Bank of the United States a never-failing source of that capital which is so essential to their prosperity and which they can get nowhere else, prepared to lend their aid in drying up the fountain of their own prosperity? Is there any class of the people or any section of the Union so lost to every sentiment of common prudence, so regardless of all the principles of Republican government, as to place in the hands of the Executive Department the means of an irresponsible and unlimited issue of paper-money—in other words, the means of corruption without check or bounds? If such be in fact the wishes of the people, they will act with consistency and propriety in voting for General Jackson as President of the United States, for by his re-election all these disastrous effects will certainly be produced. He is fully and three times over pledged to the people to negative any bill that may be passed for rechartering the bank, and there is little doubt, that the additional influence which he would acquire by a re-election would be employed to carry through Congress the extraordinary substitute which he has repeatedly proposed."

This address, although partisan at the time, contains facts, arguments, and sentiments which never were and never could be shaken, but which, in the presence of Democratic ranks, led by such a man as Benton, were like straws pitched against a mountain. They may, nevertheless, be counted as a. voice from the Democratic wilderness, from which men and politicians should profit at this day. "The official counsellors" referred to meant Jackson's regular Cabinet, a majority of whom were known to be favorable to the recharter of the bank, but it was equally well-known that Jackson had, besides these "official counsellors," what was known as his "kitchen cabinet," of whom Benton was the head and front. In fact Benton was Senator, and acted in the capacity of prophet, chief adviser of the President, defender of the Democratic faith and practice, and the Thersites or tongue-stabber of all who dared to question Jackson's infallibility. We may say that he carried the entire Democratic party and the Democratic government upon his shoulders, and would, under different circumstances, have plunged the country, as did Pericles of old, into irretrievable ruin. As it was, booted and spurred, with whip in hand he drove the entire ignorant portion of the people against the bank and a national currency. He, figuratively speaking, opened a political canyon in the midst of the land, and led or drove the people, like a herd of buffaloes, until they found themselves precipitated headlong into the terrible gulf.

"The other institution recommended as a substitute for the bank" was the same that ripened under Democratic hands into an independent treasury, which had power to issue circulating and other kinds of notes, and which thereby constituted a bank pure and simple, in the management of which the citizens, rich or poor, have no direct voice; the political powers and dangers of such an institution were a thousand-fold greater than ever could come from a bank, the stock of which is held and managed by citizens. This plan of Jackson and the Democracy, afterward supplemented by Benton's hard-money, and so-called anti-bank policy, being similar to the recent greenback theory, would, if fully carried out, rob the citizens generally, except as menials, of any part or lot in this great and leading branch of commerce, and vest the entire finances of the country, and the hundreds of millions in the Treasury of the United States, in the hands of ambitious and unscrupulous politicians, such as a Democratic party is but too

apt to develop and follow ; or, in other words, in the
hands of another "kitchen cabinet" with a Benton
at its head. Woe to our country, woe to civil
liberty on the North American continent, when
such a party again gets complete control of our
national Treasury, and its tremendous facilities for
manufacturing paper-money, with no wiser or
better statesmen than Jackson, Benton, Van Buren,
and Marcy, or their legitimate successors and representatives, such as Benjamin F. Butler and other
modern greenbackers, to manage the national
machinery !

CHAPTER XVIII.

As already stated in former chapters, the first
Bank of the United States was chartered in 1791,
under the sanction of Washington. It ran its course
and served the country with great efficiency and
benefit for twenty years, and expired in 1811. The
Jeffersonian, State-sovereignty Democracy being
then in the ascendant, the charter was not renewed at
that time. But in 1816, after a season of wreck and
ruin for the want of such an institution, a new bank
as a matter of necessity was established, and became
the chief instrument of the success and prosperity
which followed. It was upon the question of the
renewal or extension of this charter that the powers
of ignorance *vs.* the powers of intelligence, the
powers of ambition *vs.* the powers of patriotism, the
powers of retrogression *vs.* the powers of progress,
came into conflict, led on the one side by such men
as Benton, Jackson, and Amos Kendall, and on the
other by such men as Albert Gallatin, Henry Clay,
and Daniel Webster. The bill for the recharter was
introduced in January, 1832. Its friends discussed
it on the grounds of reason, logic, and the industrial
and commercial necessities of the country. Benton
and his party assailed it with pretended but base-

less accusations against its integrity and patriotism, with coarse and vulgar appeals to ignorance and depravity; and so incessant were their appeals and denunciations, and so widely were they circulated by means of government funds and facilities, something like a popular "hue-and-cry" was raised against the bank among the most ignorant portion of the people. This was the outcome of the plot conceived and matured in Jackson's "kitchen cabinet," without the approval of his regular Cabinet, a majority of whom were in favor of rechartering the bank. The bill was at length passed through both branches of Congress, by 28 votes to 20 in the Senate, and by 106 to 84 in the House of Representatives. Several Democratic members in each House, who had not yet been overawed by Benton's ribaldry or Amos Kendall's infamous calumnies, voted for the bill.

The veto of the Bank Bill by Jackson was dated July 10, 1832, and although it was expected by some persons, but few believed he would venture on so fearful a step. The intelligent portion of the people were filled with amazement and indignation. Hundreds of public meetings were held to discuss and condemn the audacious act. Business and industries of every kind were greatly shocked and disturbed, and so great was the paralysis, and so great was the consternation in all ranks, that many prominent supporters of Jackson denounced him as a tyrant, and took sides against his re-election to his second term. The message, although written with great care, was the most demagogical, sophistical, and absurd document that ever came from the head of a nation.   Its chief complaint was against the institution as a monopoly, and would as well apply to every corporation and every wealthy citizen, and to any enterprise undertaken for the development of the country, as to a Bank of the United States. Its logic, if any it contained, would, if applied to any of our railroad corporations and banks of to-day, sequestrate their assets, whenever they might call for a renewal of their charters, and invest them in the hands of other parties.   Instead of such a document tending to diminish monopoly, it operated to create one grand despotism in the hands of a Democratic President, and a host of other monopolies for plundering and oppressing the people almost beyond endurance, as we shall soon see. As can be perceived by any one who will take the trouble to read the message, it treated the bank as a free State would treat an army of occupation stationed in its midst by a foreign prince to govern the people.   No one who esteems his reputation for common sense and common understanding of the rights of property and the Constitution could be found at this day to sanction the document and the positions it assumed.

Yet Benton, Kendall, and other henchmen of Jackson soon rallied with long speeches and long articles defending the veto, and glorifying its author as the greatest man that ever lived, and denouncing the friends of the bank as the greatest rascals that ever lived.   This foul literature and these foul arguments were circulated in tons by the government, and soon brought back loud and long shouts for the conquer-

ing hero. The reciprocal action and re-action, together with hickory poles and flaunting banners
stuck up at every cross-road, and venal orators in
every nook and corner of the country repeating the
trash put forth at the Capitol, soon raised a Democratic furor that carried Jackson into his second term
as President of the United States, and equipped him
with absolute authority to press forward in other
despotic acts. Then followed the series of disasters
which he and his henchmen, Kendall, Benton, and
others, engineered under the name of victories over
what they called monopolies, monopolists, and mon-
archists, until the sad catastrophe was reached.

But let us now give some more apt and forcible illustrations of the calamities influenced and brought upon
the country by these mad partisans and their reckless acts. This is best done by quoting from those
who opposed them and did all they could to prevent
the great crime of plunging a great nation into almost
irretrievable ruin.

On the very day, the tenth of July, that the veto
message was handed into the Senate, that grand old
statesman and patriot, Henry Clay, rose and delivered
an address, exposing in a masterly manner its sophis-
tries and disorganizing sentiments. The words of
Mr. Clay, whether in a party struggle or otherwise,
whether in a heated conflict of debate or in calmer
times, stood, and will continue to stand, as a model
of political philosophy and sound advice. He closed
his speech as follows :

"Mr. President : We are about to close one of
the longest and most arduous sessions of Congress

under the present Constitution; and when we return
among our constituents, what account of the operations of their government shall we be bound to com-
municate? We shall be compelled to say, that the
Supreme Court is paralyzed, and the Missionaries
retained in prison in contempt of its authority, and
in defiance of numerous treaties and laws of the
United States; that the Executive, through the
Secretary of the Treasury, sent to Congress a tariff
bill which would have destroyed numerous branches
of our domestic industry and been the final destruction
of all; that the veto has been applied to the Bank
of the United States, our only reliance for a sound
and uniform currency; that the Senate has been
violently attacked for the exercise of a clear constitutional power; that the House of Representatives
has been unnecessarily assailed; and that the
President promulgated a rule of action for those who
have taken the oath to support the Constitution of
the United States, that must, if there be practical
conformity to it, introduce general nullification, and
end in the absolute subversion of the government."

The following was from Hon. J. M. Clayton, the
great Whig senator from Delaware:

"I ask, What is to be done for the country? All
thinking men must now admit that, as the present
bank must close its concerns in less than four years,
the pecuniary distress, the commercial embarrass-
ments, consequent upon its destruction, must exceed any thing which has ever been known in our
history, unless some other bank can be established to
relieve us. Eight and a half millions of the bank

capital, belonging to foreigners, must be drawn from us to Europe. Seven millions of the capital must be paid to the government, not to be loaned again, but to remain, as the President proposes, deposited in a branch of the Treasury, to check the issues of the local banks. The immense available resources of the present institution, amounting, as it appears by the report in the other House, to $82,057,483, are to be used for banking no longer, and nearly fifty millions of dollars in notes, discounted on personal and other security, must be paid to the bank. The State banks must pay over all their debts to the expiring institution, and curtail their discounts to do so, or resort, for the relief of their debtors, to the old plan of emitting more paper, to be bought up by speculators at a heavy discount."

We now quote some words of wisdom and warning from ' the great logician, the profound reasoner, and the defender of the Constitution ; Mr. Webster said :

" Mr. President: We have arrived at a new epoch. We are entering on experiments with the government and the Constitution of the country, hitherto untried, and of fearful and appalling aspect. This message calls us to the contemplation of a future which little resembles the past. Its principles are at war with all that public opinion has sustained, and all which the experience of the government has sanctioned. It denies first principles. It contradicts truths heretofore received as indisputable. It denies to the judiciary the interpretation of law, and demands to divide with Congress the origination of

statutes. It extends the grasp of Executive preten-
sion over every power of the government. But this
is not all. It presents the Chief Magistrate of
the Union in the attitude of arguing away the
powers of the government over which he has been
chosen to preside; and adopting for this purpose,
modes of reasoning which, even under the influence
of all proper feeling toward high official station, it
is difficult to regard as respectable. It appeals to
every prejudice which may betray men into a mistaken view of their own interests; and to every passion which may lead them to disobey the impulses
of their understanding. It urges all the specious
topics of State rights, and national encroachment,
against that which a great majority of the States have
affirmed to be rightful, and in which all of them have
acquiesced. It sows, in an unsparing manner, the
seeds of jealousy and ill-will against that government of which its author is the official head. It
raises a cry that liberty is in danger, at the very
moment when it puts forth claims to power heretofore unknown and unheard of. It affects alarm for
public freedom, when nothing so much endangers
that freedom as its own unparalleled pretences.
This even is not all. It manifestly seeks to influence
the poor against the rich. It wantonly attacks whole
classes of the people, for the purpose of turning
against them the prejudices and resentments of other
classes. It is a state paper which finds no topic too
exciting for its use; no passion too inflammable for
its address and solicitation. Such is the message.
It remains, now, for the people of the United States

to choose between the principles here avowed and their government. These cannot subsist together. The one or the other must be rejected. If the sentiments of the message shall receive general approbation, the Constitution will have perished even earlier than the moment which its enemies originally allowed for the termination of its existence. It will not have survived to its fiftieth year."

The Constitution did "perish" so far as Jackson's crew of advisers and prompters could destroy it. But fortunately there was behind it and the government itself, and beyond the reach of this Democratic crew, a conservative and enduring power, which even a Webster, with his deep research, could not fully forecast and comprehend, as experience demonstrated, the continued assaults and warfare of the Democratic party to the contrary notwithstanding. But the great questions of to-day are: Was there ever any other Constitution and government that so long stood the assaults of such a party and such a crew in possession of supreme power, without a thorough and destructive revolution? And, secondly: Can our Constitution and government ever stand and survive another such Democratic siege?

CHAPTER XIX.

THE REMOVAL OF THE DEPOSITS.

AT the time the bill for the recharter of the bank was passed in Congress, and vetoed by Jackson, the old charter had four years to run before it expired. By the laws of Congress, and, in fact, by the charter itself, the funds of the government, amounting in those days to about ten million dollars, were required to be deposited in the vaults of the bank and its branches, then numbering twenty-five, in various parts of the country, unless the Secretary of the Treasury should deem the funds unsafe. In such a case, he was authorized to remove them to places of greater security, and make immediate report to Congress, and not to the President. The President, as is the case to-day, had no legal authority or control over the funds. He could not legally draw a single dollar from them on his own order or warrant, nor had he any legal authority to transfer a single dollar from one place to another. But during the Congress of 1832 and '33, the session following Jackson's election to his second term, it being noised about that he contemplated seizing upon the deposits, with or without law, by virtue of his popularity and strength with the Democracy, on the 2d of March, 1833, the House of Representatives considered the subject, and by a vote of 110 to 46 (over two to one) resolved "that the government deposits may, in the opinion of the House, be safely continued in the Bank of the United States."

Almost any man with common sense and common honesty would suppose that with such laws in force, and such a resolution from the House of Representatives, where all government money and financial questions have their rightful consideration and solution, the President ought to have been willing to let such questions take their legitimate course. But not so. Nor was this all. When the plot of seizing upon the deposits had been concocted in Jackson's "kitchen cabinet," he brought the subject before his regular Cabinet. Here he found all, except one or two,—Roger . B. Taney, the Attorney-General, in particular,—opposed to so fearful an experiment, so fearful a crime. But it had been settled in the "kitchen cabinet," where Benton was the "head centre," and where Amos Kendall and F. P. Blair were lieutenants, that the project was to be carried out. And here we may almost as readily imagine the conversation that took place, when Jackson broached the subject to his regular Cabinet, as though we had been present to report the same. "First," says Mr. McLane, "the act of removal would be violative of the laws of Congress, and besides, the recent resolution of the House of Representatives takes from the President all responsibility in the matter." "Yes, Mr. President," says Mr. Woodbury, "this would be a fearful undertaking. It would surely bring upon the country all the disturbances and calamities predicted by Clay, Webster, and Clayton to come from the veto of the Bank Bill; and besides, there is no suitable place or places for the deposit of the public funds, except the Bank of the United States and its branches. And besides this, too, it devolves upon Congress, and not upon the President, to provide places of deposit when the charter and privileges of the present bank shall expire. Again, we had better suffer the loss of the entire amount, than to have the laws violated in the person of the Executive head of the government. And again, the President has no legal control over the public funds. The Secretary of the Treasury is alone invested with the power, and he acts only as the agent of the Congress, and is bound to report his acts immediately to Congress for their approval or disapproval." "Yes," says Mr. Duane, then Secretary of the Treasury, "I have been considering this project, at the request of the President, for some time, and I have come to the conclusion to have nothing to do with so violent and dangerous a measure." "Well, gentlemen," says Jackson, "I am sorry to differ with you, and have you differ with me, in so important a step, but, ' by the Eternal!' I am going to fight that bank as long as there is any thing to fight, law or no law, let the consequences be what they may." "Yes," says Mr. Roger B. Taney, "Gen. Jackson is right, and I am the man to help carry out his wishes in the genuine Democratic style, let the consequences take care of themselves. When Democracy has spoken, as it did in Jackson's recent re-election to the Presidency, I regard it as a warrant for any thing and every thing

that may be desired by the party. Such a victory
takes the place of all other law, as in the case with a
victory in war. The voice of the Democracy, when
it speaks, is not only the voice of the people but the
voice of God. Its mission is not to follow timid and
cautious statesmen, but some leader that is bold and
audacious. Democracy means a freshet, a flood, or a
cyclone, which no man can resist. I propose to move
with it, and hold to it, if the government breaks into
fragments, and sinks back into barbarism." This is
substantially the conversation that took place at the
regular Cabinet meeting, when Jackson first broached
his project for the removal of the deposits.

But there was another—"the kitchen cabinet"—
in which probably before and after this regular
meeting the conversation ran as follows : " Yes, Mr.
Benton," says Jackson, " I have carefully read and
considered all your speeches against the bank and
on all financial questions, and especially your hard-
money doctrine, your gold and silver currency,—the
currency of the fathers and the Constitution,—and I
am determined to tear that —— institution up by
the roots, if the heavens fall. Mr. ———, Mr.
———, Mr.———, and Mr.——— may go to ——;
I shall take the responsibility of this great act."
" Yes," said Blair, one of the "kitchen cabinet,"
" Mr. Taney is right ; the rank and file of the
Democracy, after much labor, much expenditure of
money and brains, and thanks to your military fame,
Mr. President, has been consolidated, and is now
ready for any thing, even for a war with France, or
for the overthrow of the Constitution and govern-

ment itself, if need be. Your voice is law, and a million of men are ready to come at a blast of your horn." "Yes," says Benton, "they call you the grand old hero of the battle of New Orleans, and the Herculean slayer of the Bank of the United States,—that great and corrupt monopoly, that great monarchical instrument, that *whelp* of the Bank of England, which stands in the onward path of Democracy as an obstacle to its consummation. Drive ahead, drive ahead, Mr. President; I will stand by you. I engage to keep the ranks of Democracy closed up, and on your side. I know exactly how to tickle their fancy with apt epithets and metaphors, with captivating prophecies and promises and thundering denunciations against our opponents. Or, if I should come short at any point, here are Kendall and Blair, who can turn the waste-spout of the kitchen upon Clay, Webster, and Clayton, and even Wm. C. Preston, of South Carolina, and cover them out of sight with filth. In all this matter, therefore, the Democracy will have nothing to do but to enjoy the fun, and shout for your 'Excellency.' Yes, Mr. President, go ahead; we have already secured Mr. Van Buren to be on your side and help fight the battle. Yes, sir, throttle the monster at once, while we seize it by the legs. Kendall by one leg, Blair by another, Taney by another, and Van Buren will hold the bridle until the Democracy lands him in the Presidential chair to receive your mantle. England, Russia, Prussia, and Austria seizing upon the horse of Napoleon, after the battle of Waterloo, formed a spectacle not more

sublime and animating than you and your friends
will present to the world in this warfare with the
bank and Nick Biddle, sir." After a great amount
of twaddle and talk of this kind, and after trifling
with the vast interests of the country, as if it were a
theatrical stage, and the people stage-players, and
as if their great interests were as chaff, and the animosities and ambitions of certain individuals were
the wheat, Jackson ordered Mr. Duane, the Secretary of the Treasury, to change the government deposits, then averaging about ten million dollars, from
the Bank of the United States and its branches to
certain State banks designated by himself. This
order Duane refused to obey, whereupon Jackson
removed him from office, and appointed Roger B.
Taney, a more pliant instrument, in his place.
Taney at once showed that he was ready for that or
any other Democratic edict. Hence, on the 22d of
September, 1833, the order was issued for the change
to be made, and funds to be drawn as fast as possible
from the Bank of the United States. And although
threats and rumors of mobs and insurrections were
in circulation, in case this bold and audacious course
was adopted, nothing of the kind took place, but it
is impossible for words to convey an idea of the consternation and panic that followed.

Benton had been for some time preaching up his
so-called gospel of hard money, and his crusade
against all banks and paper currency, and as most people, and even the State banks, knew his potency with
Jackson, and feared that Democracy would soon
sweep all banks from the land, and as there were but

a few million dollars of specie in the country, every body supposed that manufacturing industries and commerce must soon be reduced to a mere fraction of what then existed, and hence the panic and consternation among all classes of people, which were increased by the fear of disturbance and tumults, which have always followed a reign of Democracy in every other country. But Jackson and some of his advisers, seeing this dangerous state of affairs, soon came forward with the announcement that the several States must charter more banks to supply the vacuum caused by the overthrow of the Bank of the United States and its branches, and that the pet banks (so-called) which had received the public deposits must be liberal with their discounts to the people. These suggestions were, as a matter of course, followed by the pet banks; and nearly all the States, in their next legislative sessions, chartered new banks, *ad libitum*, and hundreds of millions of paper currency were issued by them, which the people, as a matter of course, and a matter of necessity, received with avidity. This flood of bank-notes had the effect to revive business, such as it was, after a while, and to stimulate a rage for speculation and an inflation of prices such as had never before been witnessed in any country in time of peace.

But even this reaction from the terrible depression consequent upon the veto and the removal of the deposits, was by no means sudden: the shock and paralysis of business were too great and wide-spread to be cured, if cured they could be, by any such crazy and hazardous remedies. It was at least two years before business began to recover, and when it did recover, it came with a craze and vengeance, which ran every thing and everybody wild. Flour that had been down to three and four dollars a barrel soon went up to ten and twelve dollars, meat that had been at six and seven cents a pound went up to eighteen and twenty cents a pound, and other things fluctuated in proportion. And here too we come to the fact and experience that from the reduction of the tariff, and the inflation of the prices of every thing in our country, foreign goods were imported to such an extent, that hardly a dollar of gold or silver could be found in circulation, owing to the drain of specie to pay for imports. Every kind of merchandise during the years of 1835 and '36 seemed to rest upon stilts, and as a bubble ready to burst at any moment. But it was this Democratic froth and endorsement of Jackson and Benton that enabled Mr. Van Buren to slip into the Presidency in 1836 and '37, and thus perpetuate a Democratic reign. Had not Jackson, either through fear or prudence, abandoned Benton's hard-money theory, for the time being, and turned to the State banks for help, it is to be presumed that our country would have been delivered from the curse of Democracy at that time, either by the aid of Judge Lynch or by the ballot-box in 1836. As it was, Van Buren reached the Presidency but by the skin of his teeth, even with Jackson's endorsement and popularity to aid him.

In the next chapter we will give the reader some authoritative accounts of the first crop of disasters produced by the Democratic reign, leaving the account of the terrible crash of 1837 for subsequent chapters.

CHAPTER XX.

THE Bank of the United States had a capital of thirty-five million dollars, seven million of which belonged to the government. Its circulating notes averaged about fifty million dollars, and its line of discounts ran from seventy to eighty million dollars. As before remarked, the government used the bank and its branches as places of deposit, which fund on hand usually amounted to about ten million dollars. The deposits of the mercantile community with the bank probably amounted to as much as those of the government. When, therefore, the government deposits were suddenly withdrawn from the bank by the President, as a matter of course private deposits were also withdrawn, thus inflicting a terrible blow upon the institution, as well as upon the industrial and mercantile community, inasmuch as the bank and its branches were compelled to withhold and shorten their accommodations to the people, while the State banks were also driven to the necessity of shortening their sails. At that time the population of the United States was less than fourteen million, and the purchasing power of money was more than twice as great as at the present time. Gold and silver were very scarce, and were being rendered still scarcer by the policy and course of Jackson and his "kitchen cabinet," and hence we may come to the conclusion that the depressing effect of this policy upon the country could not be excelled or equalled at the present time by the sudden abolition of all the national banks and the withdrawal of one half the greenbacks from circulation. It was not only the banks that were crippled and frightened, but all capitalists and financiers, except professional swindlers, were driven from the markets. It is not strange, therefore, that this policy and despotism of Democracy, in the person of its chiefs, produced at first great alarm, then a panic, then a paralysis in all branches of business and industry, such as had never before been witnessed in time of peace.

Benton has written and compiled two immense volumes to vindicate and extol himself and Jackson, but had he lived a hundred years longer, and produced a hundred more volumes, he could never begin to atone for the calamities they brought upon the country, or have shielded these, their mad acts, from the bitter scorn and righteous condemnation of mankind. But we must now let those who were on the spot, those who saw and tasted the bitter dose, those who saw and felt the pelting storm raised by a wicked crew of Democratic politicians, speak for themselves. It is true no men or set of men can be found to-day to stand up and defend these acts of the Democratic party and its leaders, or to contend that the support given to the bank and other Whig measures, by the Whigs, was merely partisan, or in any respect venal or wrong. No such calumny can now find consumers or admirers, but the time

has come when the entire country, the entire
people, and whole world, must look upon the policy
and acts of the Democratic party and its leaders of
those days as a base and criminal warfare against
the best interests of the people and against modern
civilization and progress.   It is on account of these
acts, facts, and fearful results, that the following
parts of speeches, made by great statesmen at that
time, cannot be too often reproduced for the consideration of the American people.

Soon after the Congress following the removal of
the public deposits had met, Mr. Clay arose in the
Senate, and commenced his review of the acts as
follows :

"We are in the midst of a revolution, hitherto
bloodless, but rapidly tending toward a total change
of the pure Republican character of the government,
and to the concentration of all power in the hands of
one man.   The powers of Congress are paralyzed,
except when exerted in conformity with his will,
by frequent and an extraordinary exercise of the
Executive veto, not anticipated by the founders of
our Constitution, and not practised by any of the
predecessors of the present Chief Magistrate.   And,
to cramp them still more, a new expedient is springing into use, of withholding altogether bills which
have received the sanction of both houses of Congress, thereby cutting off all opportunity of passing
them, even if, after their return, the members should
be unanimous in their favor.   The constitutional
participation of the Senate in the appointing power
is virtually abolished by the constant use of the

power of removal from office, without any known
cause, and by the appointment of the same individual to the same office, after his rejection by the
Senate. How often have we, Senators, felt that the
check of the Senate, instead of being, as the Constitution intended, a salutary control, was an idle
ceremony? How often, when acting on the case of
the nominated successor have we felt the injustice
of the removal? How often have we said to each
other: Well, what can we do? the office cannot remain vacant, without prejudice to the public interest,
and if we reject the proposed substitute, we cannot
restore the displaced, and perhaps some more unworthy man may be nominated?

" The judiciary has not been exempt from the
prevailing rage for innovation. Decisions of the
tribunals, deliberately pronounced, have been con-
temptuously disregarded, and the sanctity of numerous treaties openly violated. Our Indian
relations, coeval with the existence of the government, and recognized and established by numerous
laws and treaties, have been subverted, the rights of
the helpless and unfortunate aborigines trampled in
the dust, and they under subjection to unknown
laws, in which they have no voice, promulgated in
an unknown language. The most extensive and
most valuable domain that ever fell to the lot of one
nation, is threatened with a total sacrifice. The
general currency of the country—the life-blood of all
its business—is in the most imminent danger of
universal disorder and confusion. The power of
internal improvement lies crushed beneath the veto.

The system of protection of American industry was
snatched from impending destruction at the last
session ; but we are now coolly told by the Secretary
of the Treasury, without a blush, that it is understood to be *conceded on all hands*, that the tariff
for protection merely, is to be finally abandoned.
By the 3d of March, 1837, if the progress of innovation continues, there will be scarcely a vestige re-
maining of the government and its policy, as they
existed prior to the 3d of March, 1829. In a
term of eight years, a little more than equal to that
which was required to establish our liberties, the
government will have been transformed into an elective monarchy—the worst of all forms of government."

This extract is only the exordium of a long and
powerful speech in the defence of the Constitution
and laws of the country, and denunciatory of the
despotic power exercised in the vetoes of the Internal Improvement Bill, the Bank Bill, the removal
of the deposits, and other despotic acts. There is,
there was, no ground to question the profound
patriotism and honesty of the great American
Commoner, in his efforts against these destructive
measures. But as it was, the speeches of this
great statesman had no more effect on the ignorant and depraved masses of the Democratic
party and the depraved leaders thereof, than
Cicero's philippics against Antony had upon him
and his soldiers, or the speeches of St. Paul upon
the Jewish Rabbis and the rabble at their heels.
Such was the demoralization the Democratic party

had produced. As a matter of course, the main parts of this speech must be omitted here, but the whole can be found and read with profit in the "Life and Speeches of Henry Clay," vol. 2, p. 145. In regard to the bank itself, he said:

" The bank has been the constant object for years of vituperation and calumny. It has been assailed in every form of bitterness and malignity. Its operations have been misrepresented; attempts have been made to destroy its credit, and the public confidence in its integrity and solidity; and the character of its officers has been assailed. Under these circumstances, it has dared to defend itself. It has circulated public documents, speeches of members of Congress, reports made by chairmen of committees, friends of the administration, and other papers. As it was necessary to make the defence commensurate with the duration and extensive theatre of the attack, it has been compelled to incur a heavy expense to save itself from threatened destruction. It has openly avowed, and yet avows, its right and purpose to defend itself. All this was known to the last Congress. Not a solitary material fact has been since disclosed. And when before, in a country where the press is free, was it deemed criminal for any body to defend itself?"

As a sample of the financial ability and honesty of Jackson and his gang of advisers, and the institutions which they selected for the keeping of the government funds, Mr. Clay refers in his speech to the Bank of the Metropolis in Washington, of which bank the managers and stockholders were some

THE BANK OF THE UNITED STATES. 161

of Jackson's personal pets, who shared largely in the
millions of dollars plundered from the government
under this Democratic regime. He said:

" Let us look into the condition of one of these
local banks, the nearest to us, and that with respect
to which we have the best information. The banks
of this District (and among them that of the
Metropolis) are required to make annual reports
of their condition on the 1st day of January. The
latest official returns from the Metropolis bank is of
the 1st of January, 1832. Why it did not make one
on the 1st of last January, along with the other
banks, I know not. In point of fact, I am informed
it made none. Here is its account of January, 1832,
and I think you will agree that it is a Flemish one.
On the debit side stand capital paid in, five hundred
thousand dollars. Due to the banks, eighty-three
thousand seven hundred and ninety-six dollars and
ten cents; individuals on deposit, seventy-four thousand nine hundred and seventy-seven dollars and
forty-two cents; dividend and expenses, seventeen
thousand five hundred and ninety-one dollars and
seventy-seven cents; and surplus, eight thousand one
hundred and thirty-one dollars and two cents: making an aggregate of six hundred and eighty-four
thousand four hundred and ninety-six dollars and
thirty-one cents.[1] On the credit side there are bills
and notes discounted, and stock (what sort?) bearing
interest, six hundred and twenty-six thousand and
eleven dollars and ninety cents; real estate, eighteen

---

[1] " Life and Speeches of Henry Clay," vol. 2, pp. 187, 188. Published by Robert B. Bixby and Co., New York, 1843.

thousand four hundred and four dollars and eighty-
six cents; notes of other banks on hand and checks
on the same, twenty-three thousand two hundred
and thirteen dollars and eighty cents; specie—now,
Mr. President, how much do you imagine? Recollect that this is the bank selected at the seat of
government, where there is necessarily concentrated
a vast amount of public money, employed in the
expenditure of the government. Recollect that, by
another Executive edict, all public officers charged
with the disbursement of the public money here, are
required to make their deposits with this Metropolis;
and how much specie do you suppose it had at the
date of its last official return? Ten thousand nine
hundred and seventy-four dollars and seventy-six
cents; due from other banks, five thousand eight
hundred and ninety dollars and ninety-nine cents:
making in the aggregate on the credit side six hundred and eighty-four thousand four hundred and
ninety-six dollars and thirty-one cents. Upon looking into the items, and casting them up, you will find
that this Metropolis bank, on the first of January,
1832, was liable to an immediate call for one hundred and seventy-six thousand three hundred and
thirty-five dollars and twenty-nine cents, and that
the amount which it had on hand ready to meet that
call was forty thousand and seventy-nine dollars and
fifty-five cents. And this is one of the banks selected
at the seat of the general government for the deposit
of public moneys of the United States. A bank
with a capital of thirty millions of dollars and upward
of ten millions of specie on hand has been put aside,

and a bank with a capital of half a million and a little more than ten thousand dollars in specie on hand has been substituted in its place! How that half million has been raised, whether in part or in the whole by the neutralizing operation of giving stock notes in exchange for certificates of stock, does not appear."

This speech of Mr. Clay's was delivered in December, 1833, only three months after the removal had taken place. This Bank of the Metropolis, or rather its managers, shared deeply in the stupendous robberies of the government, which came to light in the explosion and crash in 1837, under Van Buren's administration. No words can so well describe the agony and horror of those times as the great Whig speeches made on the occasion. Some further extracts from these speeches will be given in future pages.

CHAPTER XXI.

THE REMOVAL OF THE DEPOSITS—CONTINUED.

THE effect of the removal of the deposits (the order for which was issued on the 22d of September, 1833) was almost instantaneous upon the business of the country, and the paralysis and agony of the people grew worse and worse for nearly two years. But no sooner had Congress assembled, than protests and denunciations of the measure flowed in from all parts of the country. Benton called the assemblies of the people to discuss the matter "distress meetings," and the memorials of Congress "distress memorials," gotten up by Whig leaders for political effect, just as if, just after the Presidential election and inauguration, nearly the whole country could be aroused to frenzy, and almost to arms, by a few private words of advice, and without some great cause; just as if a government order, which had the effect of depriving millions of people of bread, and millions of people of their wealth and honest expectations, was not calculated to arouse any people to madness. But we can let such Democratic falsehoods and slanders pass for what they are worth, since they no longer find believers. These memorials, generally accompanied by large committees of gentlemen, to present them both to the President and Congress, continued to flow in for three or four

months, so that when they were all printed, together
with the speeches made on their presentation in Congress, they comprised four closely printed volumes
of one thousand pages each.   Indeed, there was but
little done or said in Congress for four months, but
to read and comment on those memorials; and, in
fact, not until it was definitely ascertained that Jackson and his advisers would not relent of their action
did the memorials and speeches cease.

Among the many speeches which are extant, we
can only present, in this chapter, a part of one made
by Mr. Webster, on the occasion. The length of the
extract will doubtless be excused on account of its
simplicity and comprehensiveness.   It should be
recollected that there were in those days no railroads,
and that the great New York canal was the great
interior artery of trade for almost the whole country,
and hence illustrative of the whole country and its
entire interests.   Mr. Webster said:

"Mr. President: I have the honor to present to the
Senate a memorial from the city of Albany.

"New York, Philadelphia, Baltimore, and Boston
have already laid before Congress the opinions en-
tertained in those cities by men in all classes of society, and of all occupations and conditions of life,
respecting the conduct of the administration in removing the public deposits.   To these, Albany now
joins her voice,—a voice not less clear, not less strong,
not less unanimous, than that of her sister cities.

"It is well known to you, sir, and to gentlemen
on the floor of the Senate, that Albany, for its size,
is an extremely commercial city. Connected with

the sea by one of the noblest rivers on earth, it is placed, also, at a point at or near which many hundred miles of inland navigation, from the West and from the North, accumulate the products of a vast and fertile interior, and deliver them for further transport down the North River, by sailing vessels or steamers. In return for these riches of inland industry, thus abundantly poured forth to the sea, Albany receives, of course, large amounts of foreign merchandise, to be forwarded to the interior, and to be distributed for consumption in the western districts of the State, along the shores of the lakes, and even to the banks of the Mississippi itself. It is necessarily, therefore, a place of vast exchanges of property; in other words, a place of great trade.

"Albany, I believe, sir, has a population of twenty-eight or thirty thousand people. It has given, I learn, on interesting occasions, nearly, but not quite, thirty-eight hundred votes. The paper whose folds I am now unrolling, and which I have risen to present to the Chair, bears twenty-eight hundred names all believed to be qualified electors. Great pains has been taken to be accurate in this particular; and if there be a single name to this paper not belonging to a qualified voter, it is here not only by mistake, but after careful scrutiny has been had, for the purpose of avoiding such mistakes.

"Every man, sir, whose name is here, is believed to have a right to say: 'I am an American citizen; I possess the elective franchise; I hold the right of suffrage; I possess and exercise an individual share in the sovereign power of the State; I am one of those principals whose agent government is, and I expect from the government a proper regard to my interests.'

" It will thus be seen, sir, that this paper expresses the sentiments of three fourths as many citizens of Albany as have ever been collected, on any occasion, at the polls of the city. What these sentiments are, the Senate will be at no loss to understand, when the paper shall be read. Its signers possess the faculty of making themselves fully understood.

" This memorial is brought hither, for the purpose of being laid before Congress, by a committee of eighteen persons. Some of these gentlemen are well known within the walls of the Capitol, and none of them altogether unknown to members of this or the other House. They come, sir, to vouch for the general respectability of the signers to the memorial. They come to answer for them, as persons capable of perceiving, not only the general fact that recent measures of government have deranged the business of society, but of seeing also precisely how those measures have operated on their own business, their own employments, and their own prosperity.

" Unpromising, sir, as the task is; ungrateful, nay, almost hopeless as it is, this committee have not declined the wish of their fellow-citizens. They bring this solemn appeal to the notice of the two Houses of Congress. The Senate can learn from them, by personal inquiry, that there are included among the memorialists individuals of every class, occupation, employment, profession, and trade in society. The members of the committee come to make good the declarations of the memorial as to the state of things actually existing in Albany.

"Albany, sir, has been flourishing and prosperous, and seemed rapidly rising to greater and greater heights of commercial importance. There are circumstances which would appear to have favored her, and to have enabled her to stand the shock better than her neighbors. In addition to her capital, it has been understood that she was benefited in her money operations, to a considerable extent, by the use or the custody of State funds. But the Senate will not be surprised to learn, notwithstanding all her advantages, that she has not escaped the general disaster. Whatever else is to be said against the Secretary's measures, they cannot be charged with being partial in their operation. They have the merit of impartiality, inasmuch as they produce universal distress.

"Sir, our condition is peculiar. One hardly knows how to describe it. In the midst of all the bounties of Providence, and in a time of profound peace, we are poor. Our Secretary of the Treasury, sir, is not Midas. His touch does not turn every thing into gold. It seems rather to turn every thing into stone. It stops the functions and the action of organized, social life, and congeals the whole body politic. It produces a kind of instantaneous petrifaction. We still see the form of our once active social system, but it is without life ; we can trace the veins along its cold surface, but they are bloodless ; we see the muscles, but they are motionless ; the external form is yet fair and goodly, but there is a cessation of the principle of life within.

" Sir, if one could look at the state of the country at this moment, who had never heard what that " EXPERIMENT " is which the Secretary is trying, he would naturally suppose him to be some necromancer, some Prospero, who had power over the principle of action in the whole nation, and who was amusing himself by the exercise of that power, in seeing what sort of a spectacle a great, busy, stirring community would exhibit when his wand should bring all its members to a sudden pause, check them in a moment of great activity, and hold every one in the precise attitude in which he should be found when the charm begins ; as painters, though they cannot represent progressive action on the canvas, can yet represent action suddenly arrested ; or as the interior of the mountains discloses animals caught in full life and vigor, and imbedded forever in the subsiding elements of the general deluge.

" Or perhaps, sir, such a spectator might suppose that our Secretary had been imitating infantile curiosity, which thrusts its busy fingers into the opened watch for the sake of seeing how pretty its little wheels will look when they all stand still.

" But whatever a disinterested beholder might think of the manner in which the Secretary is amusing himself with 'experiments' upon the nation, the people of Albany have had quite enough of experiments. They find it efficient for every thing but good. There are some things, they admit, which it has fully proved. It has proved the rashness, the delusion, and almost the insanity of those who undertook it.

"One of the most visible effects of this measure, to the people of Albany, is its check to the growth of the city. It has been fast increasing in houses and in the number of its inhabitants. But here are persons well acquainted with the facts and circumstances who declare that the houses in course of construction this year are not one twentieth the number of last year. What is to be said in answer to that fact? The carpenter and mason are standing still with the rule and the trowel in their hands, to see when the Secretary shall have done with his experiment. Albany is a great lumber market. The very large sum of two millions of dollars is usually paid annually for this article in that city. But there is now no demand for it. The same causes operating elsewhere which operate in Albany, the timber is not wanted, can not be used, and can not be paid for. A great coasting trade is also, in ordinary times, carried on from Albany. Lumber and other articles brought down the canals are taken down the river and scattered all along the shore almost to the eastern extremity of the Union. And we all know what numbers of sloops and steam-boats usually cover the surface of the Hudson, from its mouth to Troy. Last year, as I learn, from thirty to thirty-five steam tow-boats found employment between Troy, Albany, and New York. This great extent of navigation gave wages, of course, to multitudes of industrious men, whose present power of finding employment may be judged of by the fact that six or eight of these boats are at this time adequate to the calls of commerce. The whole busi-

ness, it is said, has fallen off at least two hundred
per cent.

*　*　*　*　*　*　*　*　*

"One of the gentlemen now here is extensively
concerned in the business of transportation on the
Western and Northern canals.   He is connected
with lines which own together two hundred canal
boats, and usually employ fourteen hundred to
fifteen hundred men and as many horses.   An immediate loss of employment for at least half of this
capital and these hands is already among the consequences of the Secretary's experiment.   This
shows, sir, how the measures of government affect
wages—ay, sir, wages, the only source of the poor
man's income.   Be it remembered, that the administration is waging war for the benefit of the poor.
It has attacked the bank, laid hold of the public
treasures, disregarded the votes of Congress, and
thrown the whole country into a state of violent
excitement, out of pure sympathy for the poor, and
to protect them against the grinding power of
moneyed corporations!   Well, sir, are the poor
better off?   Are wages higher?   Is employment
more easily obtained?   Is labor more richly rewarded?   Let the Senate judge of this matter when
I state, as I am authorized to do, that men in Albany who, three months ago, were earning and receiving a *dollar and a quarter* a day, six days in the
week, are now soliciting employment for two days in
the week only, and for *sixty-two cents* a day!   And
other industrious men who were receiving a dollar a
day are now content to work for their board only.

" There is in the city a large manufacture of iron castings for stoves, hollow-ware, and machinery. Since December it is said that this manufacture has fallen off one half, and a hundred hands have been discharged in a day, most of them heads of families. If this be so, sir, and the case be but a common one, a fearful account must be running up against those who have heedlessly brought such calamities on the laboring classes.

    *   *   *   *   *   *   *   *   *

" It would be easy, sir, to run into other details and other particulars. It would be easy to follow the effects of this derangement of the currency, not only into all classes, but until we find it affecting the concerns of every individual, and touching the home comforts of every family. But such details would be only repetition. All evidence and all argument must be lost on those who do not already, from what the country exhibits on all sides, see and feel and acknowledge that the distress of the times is universal and unparalleled."

This, we repeat, is only an extract from a great address, by one of the greatest of Americans, on that fearful occasion. It contains many other points of interest, and can be found in " The Works of Daniel Webster " (vol. 4, p. 15), by those who would profit from reading the whole speech, as well as other speeches on the same occasion.

CHAPTER XXII.

BENTON tells us in his book that he made over thirty speeches during the debates over the removal of the deposits, all of which were, as a matter of course, of the swash-buckler style, and were devoured with voracious appetite by the Democracy of that day, albeit it would give one half of them at the present day the black vomit to read them. But in times when a President of the United States could appoint a government defaulter to be Secretary of State, and, as some say, forced a credit upon the books of the Treasury to render him eligible—in times when men came to Washington as poor as Pharoah's lean kine to feed upon government pap, and soon became millionnaires—in times when a President could order the entire funds of the government to be removed from place to place, upon his own responsibility, there was no difficulty in finding funds to place Benton's speeches in the hands of every man, woman, and child in the entire country, and consequently no difficulty in obtaining shouts for the conqueror of the British at New Orleans, and the slayer of the Bank of the United States, or in obtaining imprecations and howlings against such men as Adams, Clay, Webster, and Calhoun, one of whom, as some of the Democratic organs claimed, was

173

sought to be made king of America by the said bank.

Mr. Clay once said, let us have war, pestilence, and famine, rather than Gen. Jackson for President; and Benton himself once said, if Gen. Jackson should be elected President, "we shall have to legislate with pistols and dirks in our hands;" yet they both lived to see war, pestilence, and famine, and those all combined were light calamities, compared with the reign of Democracy, led by such men as Benton and Jackson.

It would appal both the senses and judgment of any readers of this day to have one tithe of the evils rehearsed that came upon the country from this reign. No pen or brush can paint the distress that ensued, first from the warfare against the bank, and thence from the wild inflation from the State banks running the country wild with speculation, thereafter to be followed by poverty and distress of ten years' duration, brought about by the crash of the State banks' currency and inflation, as recommended by Jackson.

Mr. Clay thought it proper, before the close of the great debate, to address a few personal words to Mr. Van Buren, then Vice-President of the United States, and President of the Senate, as well as heir apparent to the Democratic despotic dynasty.[1] In the Senate, Mr. Clay said:

[1] Some persons regarded this speech as a banter to Mr. Van Buren, rather than candid advice, but whether it was so or not, it contained patriotic sentiments and admonitions that ought to have been heeded by him, even then, and more especially when he became President of the United States.

" Mr. President, it is with subdued feelings of the profoundest humility and mortification that I am compelled to say, that, constituted as Congress now is, no relief will be afforded by it, unless its members shall be enlightened and instructed by the people themselves.

* * * * * * * * *

· But there is another quarter which possesses sufficient power and influence to relieve the public distress. In twenty-four hours the Executive branch could adopt a measure which would afford an efficacious and substantial remedy, and re-establish confidence. And those who, in this chamber, support the administration, could not render a better service than to repair to the Executive mansion, and, placing before the Chief Magistrate the naked and undisguised truth, prevail upon him to retrace his steps and abandon his fatal experiment. No one, sir, can perform that duty with more propriety than yourself. You can, if you will, induce him to change his course. To you, then, sir, in no unfriendly spirit, but with feelings softened and subdued by the deep distress which pervades every class of our countrymen, I make the appeal. By your official and personal relations with the President, you maintain with him an intercourse which I neither enjoy nor covet. Go to him and tell him, without exaggeration, but in the language of truth and sincerity, the actual condition of his bleeding country. Tell him it is nearly ruined and undone by the measures which he has been induced to put in operation. Tell him that *his* experiment is operating on the nation like the phil-

osopher's experiment upon a convulsed animal in an
exhausted receiver, and that it must expire in agony,
if he does not pause, give it free and sound circulation, and suffer the energies of the people to be revived and restored.   Tell him that, in a single city,
more than sixty bankruptcies, involving a loss of upward of fifteen millions of dollars, have occurred.   Tell
him of the alarming decline in the value of all property, of the depreciation of all the products of industry, of the stagnation in every branch of business,
and of the close of numerous manufacturing establishments which, a few short months ago, were in active and flourishing operation.   Depict to him, if
you can find language to portray, the heart-rending
wretchedness of thousands of the working-classes
cast out of employment.   Tell him of the tears of
helpless widows, no longer able to earn their bread;
and of unclad and unfed orphans, who have been
driven by his policy out of the busy pursuits in
which but yesterday they were gaining an honest
livelihood.   Say to him that if firmness be honorable
when guided by truth and justice, it is intimately
allied to another quality of the most pernicious tendency, in the prosecution of an erroneous system.
Tell him how much more true glory is to be won by
retracing false steps, than by blindly rushing on until his country is overwhelmed in bankruptcy and
ruin.   Tell him of the ardent attachment, the un-
bounded devotion, the enthusiastic gratitude toward
him, so often signally manifested by the American
people, and that they deserve at his hands better
treatment.   Tell him to guard himself against the

possibility of an odious comparison with that worst of Roman emperors who, contemplating with indifference the conflagration of the mistress of the world, regaled himself during the terrific scene in the throng of his dancing courtiers. If you desire to secure for yourself the reputation of a public benefactor, describe to him truly the universal distress already produced, and the certain ruin which must ensue from perseverance in his measures. Tell him that he has been abused, deceived, betrayed, by the wicked counsels of unprincipled men around him. Inform him that all efforts in Congress to alleviate or terminate the public distress are paralyzed, and likely to prove totally unavailing, from his influence upon a large portion of the members, who are unwilling to withdraw their support, or to take a course repugnant to his wishes and feelings. Tell him, that in his bosom alone, under actual circumstances, does the power abide to relieve the country; and that, unless he opens it to conviction, and corrects the errors of administration, no human imagination can conceive, and no human tongue can express, the awful consequences which may follow. Entreat him to pause, and to reflect that there is a point beyond which human endurance cannot go ; and let him not drive this brave, generous, and patriotic people to madness and despair.

*   *   *   *   *   *   *   *   *

"If I have deviated from the beaten track of debate in the Senate, my apology must be found in the anxious solicitude which I feel for the condition of the country. And, sir, if I shall have been successful in touching your heart, and exciting in you a glow of patriotism I shall be most happy. You *can* prevail upon the President to abandon his ruinous course ; and if you will exert the influence which you possess, you will command the thanks and the plaudits of a grateful people."

During the times of the bank veto and the removal of the deposits, Mr. Calhoun was standing aloof from both great parties. But seeing and feeling that the despotic acts of the administration were too threatening to be tolerated by a civilized people, he also came forward in the Senate with one of his great speeches, covering the financial condition of the country, from which the following extracts are taken :

" The Secretary alleges that the bank has interfered with the politics of the country ; if this be true, it certainly is a most heinous offence. The bank is a great public trust, possessing, for the purpose of discharging the trust, great power and influence, which it could not pervert from the object intended, to that of influencing the politics of the country, without being guilty of a great political crime. In making these remarks, I do not intend to give any countenance to the truth of the charge alleged by the Secretary, nor to deny to the officers of the bank the right which belongs to them, in common with every citizen, freely to form political principles, and to act on them in their private capacity, without permitting them to influence their official conduct. But it is strange it did not occur to the Secretary, while he was accusing and punishing the

bank on the charge of interfering in the politics of
the country, that the government also was a great
trust, vested with powers still more extensive and
influence immeasurably greater than that of the
bank, given to enable it to discharge the object for
which it was created; and that it has no more right
to pervert its power and influence into the means of
controlling the politics of the country than the bank
itself. Can it be unknown to him that the fourth
auditor of the treasury (an officer in his own department), the man who has made so prominent a
figure in this transaction, was daily and hourly med-
dling in politics, and that he is one of the principle
political managers of the administration? Can he
be ignorant that the whole power of the government
has been perverted into a great political machine,
with a view of corrupting and controlling the country? Can he be ignorant that the avowed and open
policy of the government is to reward political friends
and punish political enemies? and that, acting on this
principle, it has driven from office hundreds of honest
and competent officers for opinion's sake only, and
filled their places with devoted partisans? Can he be
ignorant that the real offence of the bank is not that
it *has* intermeddled in politics, but because it *would
not* intermeddle on the side of power? There is
nothing more dignified than reproof from the lips of
innocence, or punishment from the hands of justice ;
but change the picture—let the guilty reprove and
the criminal punish, and what more odious, more
hateful, can be presented to the imagination?

" The Secretary next tells us, in the same spirit,

that the bank has been wasteful of the public funds
that it has spent some thirty. forty. or fifty thousand
dollars—I do not remember the exact amount (trifles
have no weight in the determination of so great a
question)—in circulating essays and speeches in
defence of the institution, of which sum one fifth
part—some seven thousand dollars—belonged to the
government. Well, sir, if the bank has really *wasted*
this amount of the public money, it is a grave charge.
It has not a right to waste a single cent; but I
must say, in defence of the bank, that, assailed as it
was by the Executive, it would have been un-
faithful to its trust, both to the stockholders and
to the public, had it not resorted to every proper
means in its power to defend its conduct, and,
among others, the free circulation of able and
judicious publications.

" But admit that the bank has been guilty of
wasting the public funds to the full extent charged
by the Secretary, I would ask if he, the head of the
financial department of the government, is not
under as high and solemn obligation to take care
of the moneyed interest of the public as the bank
itself. I would ask him to answer me a few simple
questions : How has he performed his duty in relation to the interest which the public holds in the
bank? Has he been less wasteful than he has
charged the bank to have been? Has he not
wasted thousands, where the bank, even according
to his own statement, has hundreds? Has he not,
by withdrawing the deposits, and placing them in
the State banks, where the public receives not a cent

of interest, greatly affected the dividends of the Bank of the United States, in which the government, as a stockholder, is a loser to the amount of one fifth of the diminution? a sum which, I will venture to predict, will many fold exceed the entire amount which the bank has expended in its defence. But this is a small, a very small, proportion of the public loss in consequence of the course which the Executive has pursued in relation to the bank, and which has reduced the value of the shares from 130 to 108 (a senator near me says much more—it may be, I am not particular in such things), and on which the public sustains a corresponding loss on its share of the stock, amounting to seven millions of dollars—a sum more than two hundred-fold greater than the waste which he has charged upon the bank. Other administrations may exceed this in talents, patriotism, and honesty; but, certainly, in audacity, in effrontery, it stands without a parallel!"

In regard to the despotic act of removal, Mr. Calhoun said, in the same speech:

"The senator from Kentucky has given a description of Cæsar forcing himself, sword in hand, into the treasury of the Roman commonwealth. We are at the same stage of our political revolution, and the analogy between the two cases is complete, varied only by the character of the actors and the circumstances of the times. That was a case of an intrepid and bold warrior, as an open plunderer, seizing forcibly the treasury of the country, which, in that republic as well as ours, was confided to the custody of the legislative department of the government. The

actors in our case are of a different character; artful and cunning politicians, and not fearless war-
riors. They have entered the treasury, not sword in
hand, as public plunderers, but with the false keys
of sophistry, as pilferers, under the silence of mid-
night. The motive and object are the same, varied
only by character and circumstances. 'With money
I will get men, and with men money,' was the
maxim of the Roman plunderer. With money we
will get partisans, and with partisans votes, and with
votes money, is the maxim of our public pilferers.
With men and money, Cæsar struck down Roman
liberty at the battle of Pharsalia, never to rise again ;
from which disastrous hour, all the powers of the
Roman republic were consolidated in the person of
Cæsar, and perpetuated in his line. With money
and corrupt partisans, a great effort is now making
to choke and stifle the voice of American liberty,
through all its constitutional and legal organs, by
pensioning the press, by overawing the other departments, etc."

These extracts are sufficient to give a slight conception of the distress and ruin that prevailed, the
discontent and bitterness engendered by the illegal
and tyrannical acts of the administration. And it is
here safe and proper to say that under the sway of
no other than a Democratic party, and in no country
except the United States, could such political villainy
have been perpetrated, without producing an internecine war or subjecting its authors to condign
punishment.

CHAPTER XXIII.

IT is beyond the power of the pen to describe, or the imagination to conceive, the consternation and distress brought upon the country by the despotic and vandal conduct of this Democratic administration. In the midst of this distress, Benton made several of his " spread-eagle" and gasconading speeches, declaring and contending that the distress was all imaginary and gotten up by the Whig orators and newspapers, and that the situation was the same as when the first bank was wound up in 1811, which assertions and assumptions, though false, were a " good-enough Morgan " for the rank and file of the Democracy. From 1807 to 1812, Napoleon's " Berlin Decree," and the " British orders " in council, together with Jefferson's embargo, had nearly annihilated the commerce of the United States, (except such American contraband enterprises as were engaged in violating the embargo and running the French and British blockades,) thereby cutting off the necessity for all or nearly all bank accommodations. During those years business was nearly at a standstill from these causes. Hence, says one of the best authorities, " Appleton's Cyclopedia," " the bank was now obliged to wind up its affairs, which was done without at all convulsing the country." Although Benton claimed all the while to be a hard-money man, he saw as clearly as any one, that in tearing the Bank of the United States and its branches up by the roots, great havoc must be worked in all branches of industry and commerce. Hence it was that in Jackson's Bank veto message, which he unquestionably helped to compose, and then in the order for the removal of deposits, which, he informs us, he drafted with his own hand, it was given out that such State banks as were in existence must be liberal in their accommodations to the public, and that the State governments must also be liberal in granting new charters. This policy, it was claimed, would supply the place of the Bank of the United States and its branches, as they were being crushed out ; a theory which had in it about as much reason and sense as would a plan for closing up all the old factories of the country, and inviting new ones to take their places. An important part of the plot was for the State banks receiving the deposits to inflate the currency and loans to the greatest possible extent.

These recommendations and influences—the influence of ten millions of dollars to be had without interest—coming, as they did, from the Executive department of the general government, were too potent not to be accepted by prudent business men, and made effective through the cupidity, avarice, and speculative spirit, which is ever ready to spring into activity in all commercial communities. The result was that the State-bank currency was greatly inflated, and all the State governments in the hands of the Democratic party granted bank charters almost

without a limit. In New York, Pennsylvania, and
Ohio, and, in fact, in nearly all the States, except those
of New England, charters were granted to all who
applied, and even the then Whig State of Kentucky
—where, as Mr. Clay tells us, they had only one bank
of limited capital—was seized with the mania, and
the Legislature granted charters to the amount of
ten million dollars; thus was the number of bank
charters in the United States more than doubled, in
compliance with Executive recommendations, in less
than two years after the removal of the deposits.
The alarm among prudent business men was very
great, but no words and no action could arrest the
tidal wave of inflation that had been put in motion
by the administration. Among the hundreds of
warnings and predictions that were given at that
time, as the plot was being unfolded, we can only
present one by Mr. Webster, delivered in the Senate,
in January, 1834, and less than four months after the
removal of the deposits. He said:

"I have already endeavored to warn the country
against irredeemable paper; against the paper of
banks which do not pay specie for their own notes;
against that miserable, abominable, and fraudulent
policy which attempts to give value to any paper, of
any bank, one single moment longer than such paper
is redeemable on demand in gold and silver. I wish
most solemnly and earnestly to repeat that warning.
I see danger of that state of things ahead. I see
imminent danger that a portion of the State banks
will stop specie payments. The late measure of the
Secretary, and the infatuation with which it seems

to be supported, tend directly and strongly to that result. Under pretence, then, of a design to return to a currency which shall be all specie, we are likely to have a currency in which there shall be no specie at all. We are in danger of being overwhelmed with irredeemable paper, mere paper, representing not gold nor silver; no, sir, representing nothing but broken promises, bad faith, bankrupt corporations, cheated creditors, and ruined people."

But this and a thousand other warnings from the Whigs did no good; the ball had been set in motion by the vandal policy, and nothing could stop it until it reached the bottom of the hill and pit of destruction. The spirit of avarice, the spirit of speculation, and the mania for becoming rich, without work, seized upon one half of the people, and as hard money was known to be very scarce, credit and kiting became the order of the day,--credit in the morning, credit at noon, and credit in the evening; credit upon credit, upon this side and upon that side; credit for every thing to eat, drink, and to wear, and credit in all sorts of undertakings and enterprises, and all sorts of property were bought and sold upon credit. And from this state of affairs there grew up a spirit and practice of cheating and swindling such as never had before been known in our country. The old maxims of honesty and integrity were scouted as unworthy of the times and inconsistent with Democratic liberty. Banks were established entirely upon credit, or upon nothing, the stockholders exchanging their notes with each other and counting them as cash to pay for shares, or if they had a few hard dollars in the pretended bank they were known to invent drawers, or boxes, by which the coin could be counted a dozen times over to answer the demands of the law, where such a law existed. Upon such bases bank-bills were issued by the million, and loaned to the people at high rates of interest, or paid out for the purchase of property of any and every kind to all who could be induced to sell, precisely as was done with Confederate money during the great Democratic rebellion. But even worse than this, banks in remote sections of the country colleagued with each other to exchange and circulate each other's notes. Others located their banks at inaccessible points in the country to prevent their bills from being presented for redemption. Individuals as well as banks, with or without property, gained and gave credit, until it was hard to distinguish the rich from the poor. Out of this Democratic policy and management broods of gamblers sprung into existence, and a great tribe of forgers and counterfeiters spread over the country who were never broken up until the State banks were abolished, and the entire currency was taken into the hands of the general government during the Civil War.

Commencing in 1835, the prices of every thing went up, and kept going higher and higher until the explosion of 1837 took place, when the prices of every thing went as far below the normal standard as they had gone above it. But not among the least of the evil effects of this Democratic policy was the fact that the high prices of merchandise caused immense importations of foreign products, which drew off what little gold and silver there was in the country to pay for them, thus paralyzing home industry.

Notwithstanding the rapid increase of manufacturing establishments and products from 1820 to 1832, and notwithstanding the inflation of the currency and credits, and the wide-spread speculations in all kinds of property from 1835 to 1837, during the decade from 1832 to 1840, manufactures and, in fact, all sorts of industries and productive enterprises actually declined in number and amounts, and the increase of population during the same decade was lower in its percentage than that during any decade in the history of the country, and, in fact, it was estimated by able statisticians from the best obtainable data, that the value of the entire property of the United States was diminished thirty-three per cent., or, as some estimated it, four hundred millions of dollars, the whole property, being then estimated at about twelve hundred million dollars. If we should say this Democratic policy, this Democratic experiment with the currency of the country, was worse than the "John Law Fraud" or the "South Sea Bubble," we should express nothing more than demonstrable facts. We say worse than the "John Law Fraud" or the "South Sea Bubble," because those schemes beguiled and fleeced principally the rich, while this Democratic scheme did more, first, to deprive the poor people of employment, and then to inflate the price of all the necessaries of life, to make the rich richer and the poor poorer, than any other financial humbug ever invented ; for the reason that such schemes are always used by capitalists and sharpers to increase their gains at the expense of the laboring classes. All this disorganization and robbery had, as a matter of course, to come to an end, as it did in the crash of 1837, and necessitated the calling of an extra session of Congress by President Van Buren, before he had been in office three months, to prevent universal anarchy and chaos in the land.

But before closing this chapter, it should be mentioned that Mr. Van Buren was carried into the Presidency in 1836 and '37 by two special influences incidental to a Democratic party. First by heirship to the Democratic despotism which had grown up under Jackson, and which he had inherited by his cunning, his servility, and obsequiousness to Jackson and his "kitchen cabinet," of which Benton was boss. And secondly by means of the influence of the State-bank villainy raised upon the ruins of the crushed National Bank, which villainous bubble continued to expand and to craze the people for two years, covering the period of the Presidential election of 1836, and finally burst in two months after Mr. Van Buren's inauguration. Had the explosion taken place one year earlier, it is quite probable that the country would have been rid of Democracy, as a party name and organization, and saved, in part at least, from the desolating calamities which followed in the wake of its wicked reign.

And as further data for these reflections, we may as well here give some extracts from Mr. Van Buren's message to the extra session of Congress, called by him to meet in September, 1837, on account of the great financial crash, and to prevent universal anarchy and chaos in the land. But it must be borne in mind that these admissions were rendered a necessity by the surrounding circumstances and condition of affairs, and as there were but few reliable bank statistics in those days, and the President very well knew that all this distress was the result of Democratic policy, he, as a matter of course, drew the picture as mildly and as favorably to his own party as possible. His efforts to account for them "from antecedent causes" were all sophistry, as everybody now understands. Mr. Van Buren said:

"The history of trade in the United States, for the last three or four years, affords the most convincing evidence that our present condition is chiefly to be attributed to over-action in all the departments of business; an over-action deriving, perhaps, its first impulses from antecedent causes, but stimulated to its destructive consequences by excessive issues of bank paper, and by other facilities for the acquisition and enlargement of credit. At the commencement of the year 1834, the banking capital of the United States, including that of the National Bank, then existing, amounted to about two hundred millions of dollars; the bank-notes, then in circulation, to about ninety-five millions; and the loans and discounts of the banks, to three hundred and twenty-four millions. Between that time and the first of January, 1836, being the latest period to which accurate accounts have been received, our banking capital was increased to more than two hundred and fifty-one millions, our paper circulation to more than one hundred and

forty millions, and the loans and discounts to more
than four hundred and fifty-seven millions. To this
vast increase are to be added the many millions of
credit acquired by means of foreign loans, contracted
by the States and State institutions, and, above all,
by the lavish accommodations extended by foreign
dealers to our merchants.

"The consequences of this redundancy of credit,
and of the spirit of reckless speculation engendered
by it, were a foreign debt contracted by our citizens,
estimated, in March last, at more than thirty millions
of dollars; the extension to traders in the interior of
our country of credits for supplies, greatly beyond
the wants of the people; the investment of thirty-
nine and a half millions of dollars in unproductive
public lands, in the years 1835 and 1836, while in the
preceding year the sales amounted to only four and
a half millions; the creation of debts, to an almost
countless amount, for real estate in existing or anticipated cities and villages, equally unproductive,
and at prices now seen to have been greatly dispro-
portionate to their real value; the expenditure of
immense sums in improvements, which in many cases
have been found to be ruinously improvident; the
diversion to other pursuits of much of the labor that
should have been applied to agriculture, thereby
contributing to the expenditure of large sums in the
importation of grain from Europe,—an expenditure
which amounted, in 1834, to about two hundred and
fifty thousand dollars, was in the first two quarters
of the present year increased to more than two
millions of dollars; and, finally, without enumerating

other injurious results, the rapid growth among all classes, and in our great commercial towns, of luxurious habits, founded too often on merely fancied wealth, and detrimental alike to the industry, the resources, and the morals of the people."

These extracts, significant as they are, give but a subdued and mild synopsis of the terrible condition in which the country, the government, and the people found themselves at that time. We must therefore continue the discussion of this "crash" in the next chapter.

CHAPTER XXIV.

THE CRASH OF 1837 AND THE STEPS WHICH LED TO IT.

"THE revulsion," as Mr. Van Buren modestly calls the outcome of the terrible Democratic " experiment," took place in May, 1837, two months after General Jackson's retirement from, and Mr. Van Buren's succession to, the Presidency. Instead of " revulsion " merely, it was a crash, as it has ever since been called—an explosion, that was heard and felt throughout the civilized world ; an explosion, the effects of which are almost beyond the power of words to describe, or the mind of man to measure ; an explosion, a crash, and a paralysis in industrial and business circles from which this country did not fully recover in ten years, and which produced a condition of affairs, as Mr. Van Buren was forced to acknowledge, "detrimental alike to the industry, the resources, and the morals of the people." This Benton-Jackson Democratic experiment, as a whole—that is, commencing with the veto of the Bank Bill in 1832, and ending with this crash,—was hardly less disastrous to the entire country and the whole people than is a cyclone to the belt of country over which it sweeps,—an "experiment " utterly inconsistent with civilized society, and such as never could have been hatched, concocted, or executed in any civilized country, without a Democratic party and the vices and dangers it

engenders. A barbaric or half-civilized people like
the ancient Mexicans, with their simple coins and
tokens of value, or the nations of Africa with their
cowries, might not have felt or cared for the tam-
pering of their rulers with their currency and mediums of exchange, such as they were, because they
could fall back upon their primitive modes of barter,
and might have been content ; but free people, whose
interests were identified with all the arts, discoveries,
facilities, and comforts of a thousand years among
their ancestry, could not, and ought not, to stand by
and see the choicest of these arts, facilities, and improvements of civilized life wrenched from them, and
consumed in fire and smoke, kindled and fanned by
a gang of political charlatans and hypocrites, such as
a Democratic party seems always to engender and
bring to the surface.

And here it may, and probably should, be asked, if
the old Republicans or Whigs of those days were always on the right side of all the great questions of
the day, and always had the weight of logic and argument as well as the public interests on their side,
as everybody now acknowledges they had, and the
Benton-Jackson Democracy were always on the
wrong side, and had nothing but ambition, sophistry,
passion, and prejudice to sustain them ; or, in other
words, if the Democrats were always on the wrong
side of the great questions, and had neither logic,
precedence, nor the interests of the people to uphold
them, as everybody now acknowledges was the case,
why was it and how was it, that these Democratic
leaders almost invariably carried a majority of the

voting population with them? This question, or these questions, can be answered in a few words. As before observed, ambitious, artful, and unscrupulous politicians, such as exist in all ages and countries, and are ever a standing menace to free government and equal rights, clubbed together, or, as we would say nowadays, formed themselves into a "ring" for selfish and ambitious purposes, and by impassioned speeches and other means well known to artful demagogues, were enabled to excite the people and organize into a party all or nearly all the ignorant and depraved elements of society which have always rendered the representative and equitable form of government very difficult to construct, maintain, or perpetuate. Or to state the case in other words, the Democratic politicians, under the name of Democracy, were enabled to collect into a party all or nearly all the elements—the ignorance and depravity in society—which are ever ready to help artful and unscrupulous demagogues to undermine and overthrow all rational liberty and equal rights, under the hypocritical cry of friendship for the people, albeit they are animated by nothing but selfish and ambitious aims for place and power. As some incontestable evidence of all these charges against those Democratic leaders, it may be stated that the sessions of Congress held during the administration of John Quincy Adams (from 1825 to 1829) were mainly occupied by these Democratic leaders in introducing and discussing propositions to ferret out, investigate, and expose what they called the extravagance and corruption of the administration.

Boss Benton introduced no less than six of these propositions in one day. Probably not less than fifty such were introduced, and as many committees appointed during the said four years for the same purpose, and probably not less than five hundred speeches were made upon the same subject, all of which were supplemented and garnished inside and out with "State sovereignty," the "Alien and Sedition Laws" of 1798, and overwhelming Democratic arguments to prove that such men as Adams, Clay, and Webster were bending all their energies to establish a monarchy on the ruins of the republic. And as these propositions and tactics were successful, not in finding extravagance and corruption in Adams' administration, for there were none there, but successful in lifting the Democratic party into power in 1829, this kind of political economy and management seems to have become a time-honored principle of the party in fighting its opponents and carrying its measures. And thus it happened the same party, or rather its leaders, having obtained a majority in the national House of Representatives in 1876, concluded to try the same tactics, with its thirty or forty committees and its terrible speeches against the modern Republican party; but as the people had gained somewhat in intelligence, and had become better posted as to Democratic humbuggery, the party failed in 1880 to carry the country with them, and to place their man in the Presidency.

The Bank of the United States and its branches, as heretofore stated, were established by the laws of Congress, and were constituted places of deposit for the government funds, and, as a natural consequence, became the chief places of deposit for the citizens, as well as depôts of exchange, both foreign and domestic, for the government and the people. In this way, and by means of its loans and currency, the bank and its branches had become interwoven with almost every enterprise, interest, and fibre of society. In view, then, of all these circumstances and relations, the warfare upon it, it must be confessed, was a bold and audacious one, and such as never would have been undertaken by any leaders except those of a Democratic party, and certainly never could have been crowned with success, even with a Democratic party, without a great amount of corruption, and "the cohesive power of public plunder" to hold the party intact. And is it hardly possible for any intelligent man to bring himself to the conclusion, at this time, that Gen. Jackson, after putting forth the sentiments of his first annual message, touching the great measures and policies of the fathers, could have been brought to adopt the reactionary course in respect to them which he afterward pursued. But the truth seems to be that he had become intoxicated with the reckless spirit of a Democratic party, and the audacity of the men around him. He had found how easy it was for a leader to profit by the ignorance and depravity which always lie in reserve in a Democratic party, ready to be launched against any thing great and noble, against virtue, merit, and good character; and having further learned from those around him, that a Democratic party, as such, has no

conscience, no moral sense, no consistency, no policy
or rule of action, but its own will, as expressed by
its leaders, and no idea but the blind following of
such leaders, regardless of consequences, he boldly
and recklessly embarked in the plot to overthrow the
great measures and policies of the fathers, vainly supposing, and no doubt being told by his intimate advisers, that such a course would make him a greater hero
than Washington. Even Mr. Van Buren declared that
" it was glory enough for him to have served under
such a chief."

The President, therefore, having felt the pulsa-
tions, and learned the availability of his party, was
prepared for any line of conduct. The first opportunity for the reactionary line of policy was found in
the Maysville Road Bill, passed in 1831, which,
notwithstanding the favorable terms in which he had
spoken of such measures in his first message, fell
under his veto. In accordance with his own suggestion, in the same message, the recharter of the
bank was brought forward in 1832, and having
passed in the Senate by twenty-eight to twenty,
and the House of Representatives by one hundred
and six to eighty-four, was vetoed by him, in accordance with his reactionary policy and with the wishes
of the howling political dervishes who had aroused
the prejudices of the people against the institution,
and in accordance with the instincts of. a Democratic party for attacking and uprooting any and
every thing that has been built up, whether good
or bad.   The party, being thus aroused and prepared in 1832, endorsed the Act by reëlecting him

to the Presidency for the next four years. In this
election, the party obtained the complete control of
all the offices and patronage of the government, and
the removals and appointments soon put into execution its barbaric motto, that "to the victors belong the spoils," and money speedily flowed like
water along all the veins and fibres of the organization. No such assessment of salaries, no such
plunder of the public funds, no such expensive
organizations a.id political parades had ever been seen
in our country. No such floods of documents and
speeches ever went out before. No such running
to and fro of orators and managers was ever before
witnessed. Nor, indeed, had there ever been seen
so much arrogance, so much ruffianism, so much
drunkenness and violence in an election. Benton's
arrogant speeches served everywhere as the key-
notes and political texts of the campaign. So
lavishly were the funds poured out, so thoroughly
and effectively were the gatherings, orators,
managers, and canvassers organized, that the votes
in almost all the districts were counted and tabu-
lated weeks and even months before the election
took place, the ignorance and depravity of the
voters being the chief factors and bases of the
calculations ; and, strange to say, they turned out to
be exceedingly correct when compared with the
election returns. There are at this day thousands
of living men who can attest the truth of all these
facts and charges.

And thus was achieved the greatest victory of
ignorance and vice over virtue and intelligence, of

ambition and lust of power over patriotism and
statesmanship, and of the wrong over the right, ever
witnessed in any election in a civilized community.

Jackson, having been thus carried into his second
term, was greatly elated and emboldened, and proceeded in 1833, as already repeated, to perpetrate the
most arbitrary and despotic act that could be conceived or undertaken in a country under a representative and well-organized form of government.
This consisted in the seizure of the public deposits,
and their removal from the places assigned them by
the laws of the land, and in placing them where they
were nearly all swallowed up by suspensions, defalca-
tions, and downright theft and plunder. But having
thus throttled the Bank of the United States, and
having thus cajoled and stimulated the State banks
to fill the country with unsound and irredeemable
currency, and having thus raised a tempest of wild
speculation in all kinds of property,—in a word, having
called into existence what may be called a financial
volcano, he issued, or caused to be issued, what was
called his "treasury order," or "the specie circular,"
forbidding any thing but gold and silver to be received for public lands. This was Jackson's last
card, or the last feather that broke the camel's back,
or rather the last shot to uncap the volcano which
he and his "kitchen cabinet" had caused to rise and
explode in the country.

This order, as a matter of course, the specie having
already been driven out of the country, caused the
sales of land, which had, under the spirit of speculation, run as high as twenty million dollars a year, to

cease as suddenly as if struck and silenced by the wand of a magician, and, what was quite as significant, convinced the State banks that the President had decided to turn his battle-axe against them, on account of their failure to pay specie when demanded. The result was that every bank, with or without real capital, commenced gathering into its possession all the funds and valuable property it could lay its hands on, preparatory to the crash that all now foresaw must come, and soon did come with a vengeance in 1837, in every part of the country, shaking and shivering every branch of industry, every enterprise and financial establishment from centre to circumference, and from dome to foundation.

And thus was consummated and thus was exploded, not a scheme which anybody regarded as promising a millennium in finance or as a harbinger of better times to come, but a scheme which all able and honest statesmen denounced as worse than visionary, and all honest and sensible men knew must sooner or later meet with a complete overthrow, accompanied with wide-spread ruin,—a scheme which every honest and sensible man knew at the time it was started to be the fruit of vile ambition, and to have been kept afloat more by the opportunities it afforded for robbery and public plunder than by the expectation of any benefit to come from it to the country at large,—a scheme which, as every honest and sensible man knew, found its chief support in the ignorance and depravity of the Democratic party, constantly fired up by such harangues as Benton and other leaders had prepared and placed before the party.

To say that this now exploded Benton-Jackson Democratic " experiment " was to bring poverty and ruin upon the laboring classes, and in fact upon all except a few astute capitalists and speculators; to say that it had now reached a point when the country was to be filled, as its fruits, with tramps and beggars, and when well-to-do farmers, merchants, manufacturers, and mechanics were to be driven out, like fugitives before their creditors, to seek bread and homes they knew not where; to say that the entire country and society at large were to be brought almost to a state of anarchy by this wretched " experiment," is to say nothing more than the truth, and still leave many untold calamities which words are inadequate to describe. To say that a gang of political mounte-banks and traders upon public confidence had in a time of profound peace brought a prosperous and happy country to a condition of poverty and distress, worse than is usually found in the track of an invad-ing army or a long and desolating war, is to describe no greater calamities than fell upon the entire country as the result of this Democratic "experi-ment."

To give the readers of this generation some further insight into the miseries of those days, it should be mentioned that when there are two or three kinds of currency in circulation in any country the worst always crowds the better out. Soon after the State bank inflation policy of the administration was developed, and at the time the crash came, a large portion of the bank paper afloat among the people, both of notes and bills of exchange, came

from banks mainly gotten up for swindling purposes.
With such trash the country was flooded. The explosion, as a matter of course, did much to expose the
frauds, and as almost everybody was in debt, and
creditors demanded specie or the property of their
debtors at greatly reduced prices, and as there was
no specie or further credit to be had, some conception can be formed of the misery and poverty this
wicked plot had brought upon the country, and
from the effects of which the people did not recover
in ten years, if indeed they ever did recover, until
this Democratic demoralization and disorder culminated in the great Civil War, and finally ended in a
political and financial reconstruction. And, further,
as the prices of every thing had been carried by the
inflation to an enormous height, so all kinds of property, when the crash came, sank as it were to nothing, thus adding fuel and fire to this Democratic load
of poverty and distress brought upon the people.

CHAPTER XXV.

RETROSPECT, AND COMPARATIVE PILFERINGS AND EXPEN-
DITURES OF DIFFERENT PARTIES AND AD-
MINISTRATIONS.

> " Hills peep o'er hills, and
> Alps on Alps arise."

IT is well remembered by all old men that the
leading cry and arguments employed by the Democrats against the Adams and Clay party, while they
were in power, were dishonesty, extravagance, and
corruption. These complaints and charges were carried to such an extent by speeches and investigating
committees in Congress, and by Democratic newspapers, that a majority of the people were led to believe them, and vote Gen. Jackson and his party into
power in 1828, and, indeed, in 1832. It is, therefore,
altogether proper before closing this volume to
present the reader with some comparative facts and
figures which go far to show which party was the
more dishonest, extravagant, and corrupt in handling
the public funds, and why it was and how it was that
many Democrats who came to Washington as poor
as church mice and got into high positions soon became rich. Several of them, in fact, in a short time
became millionnaires, and were able to entertain
in great splendor members of Congress and foreign
ministers.

To this end, we must quote from statistics now accessible to all, the amount of government moneys collected and disbursed by the respective parties. But first, as to the pilfering, after the funds were in hand, by the agents who handled them.

Under John Quincy Adams, as President, four years, from 1825 to 1829, the amount lost by such thievery was $885,374.

Under Andrew Jackson, as President eight years, from 1829 to 1837, the amount lost by such thievery was $3,761,112.

Under Martin Van Buren, as President four years, from 1837 to 1841, the amount lost was $3,343,792.

By these figures we see that the losses from such a source were greatly augmented under Democratic rule. They stand in point of loss on each thousand dollars as follows:

Under Adams, two dollars and seventy-five cents ($2.75) loss on the $1,000.

Under Jackson, seven dollars and fifty-two cents ($7.52) loss on the $1,000.

Under Van Buren, eleven dollars and seventy-one cents ($11.71) loss on the $1,000.

But we must now present the net amount of expenditures under the respective parties and administrations. In order to be more comprehensive, we may take two or three decades in which the respective parties were the responsible actors; first, from 1820 to 1830, when the old Republican party had the control and direction of the government, under the administrations of Mr. Monroe and Mr. Adams; and second, the decade from 1830 to 1840, under the administrations of Gen. Jackson and Mr. Van Buren. These statistics are compiled from "Appleton's American Cyclopedia," article: History of the United States, which may be counted as reliable authority as any.

Taking the decade from 1820 to 1830, we find the average population of the United States to have been eleven million two hundred and forty-nine thousand nine hundred and twenty-one (11,249,921), and taking the decade from 1830 to 1840, we find the average population to have been fourteen million nine hundred and sixty-seven thousand seven hundred and thirty-six (14,967,736).

Now the net ordinary expenditures of the government for the decade commencing in 1820 and ending in 1830 amounted to one hundred and twenty-two million dollars ($122,000,000). This amount, according to the increase and ratio of population for the decade from 1830 to 1840, should have been about one hundred and sixty-three million dollars ($163,-000,000). But instead of this corresponding amount of expenditure by the Jackson Democracy during their ten years, they disposed of two hundred and thirty million seven hundred thousand dollars ($230,-700,000), thus increasing the net ordinary expenditures sixty-seven million seven hundred thousand dollars ($67,700,000) over the average expenditure of the previous ten years, and this excessive expenditure very accurately expresses the amount of government money squandered, plundered, and stolen from the treasury of the United States by the Democratic politicians during the said ten years. The gross expenditures of the two decades, when the amount of the public debt paid in each is taken into account, show about the same difference in the amount of expenditure, or about the same amount of plunder and robbery by the Democracy.

Benton frequently boasts of the timeliness and power of his own speeches in forming public sentiment and in meeting and overthrowing the arguments of the Whig orators, and this amount of plunder, being more than five million dollars per annum, accounts for the free and wide circulation of Benton's speeches, and the certainty with which the Democratic leaders counted upon the ignorance and depravity of the country to be carried for the Democratic party, while at the same time the conscientious motives and limited fortunes of such men as Adams, Clay, Calhoun, and Webster prevented their speeches from reaching the masses of the people.

Desiring to be fair with the Democracy, and afford them credit for the benefits derived from the old Whig victory of 1840,—the benefit of which victory was in part lost by a treacherous occupant in the place of President Harrison, deceased,—and wishing to give the Democracy credit for extra expenditure growing out of the Mexican war, during the decade from 1840 to 1850, we must, therefore, in order to demonstrate that an unchecked Democratic party is always as extravagant, always as corrupt as it can possibly be, compare the expenditures of 1850 to 1860 with the old Republican party's expenditures of 1820 to 1830, as quoted above.

Men not yet very old remember that when the

lamented Harrison died, within one month after he was inaugurated President of the United States in 1841, the old Whig Congress voted his wife and family one year's salary of twenty-five thousand dollars, and that the Democratic party, or rather its leaders and managers, who had actually robbed, plundered, and stolen during the past decade more than sixty million dollars of the people's money, as shown by the figures above quoted, raised a tremendous howl, and placarded the whole country with this Whig extravagance and plunder in voting away twenty-five thousand dollars to Harrison's family for one month's service, and by their howling speeches and placards, assisted by the treachery of Harrison's successor, actually so aroused and rallied the ignorance and depravity of the country as to return to the next Congress a Democratic majority of its members. This virtually restored to the Democratic leaders the control of the government in 1843, with Benton still as boss,—and all this, we say, on account of twenty-five thousand dollars paid to the family of the lamented Harrison, in the face and eyes of more than sixty million dollars of the people's money plundered and squandered by the Democratic leaders and managers during the previous decade, as seen by the figures above given.

And, again, middle-aged men well remember that when that stern patriot and great military chieftain, Zachary Taylor, had been elected President in 1848, and died in 1849, six months after his inauguration, these same immaculate Democratic leaders, Benton excepted and now repudiated, raised another howl of extravagance and plunder on the part of the Whigs, and so aroused the ignorance and depravity of the country as to again carry the country for the Democracy, and enable the party to again take control of the government, and finally elect Franklin Pierce to the Presidency in 1852, thus making the said party responsible for the expenditures, robbery, and plunder from 1850 to 1860, which must now be compared with the old Republican party's expenditures from 1820 to 1830, as above given.

The decade of 1850 to 1860 was another period of profound peace, the usual Indian wars excepted. Consulting the same authority, "Appleton's Cyclopedia," we find the average population of that decade to have been twenty-seven million three hundred and seventeen thousand five hundred and ninety-eight (27,317,598), which, compared with the decade of 1820 to 1830, would require an expenditure of two hundred and twenty-two million six hundred thousand dollars only ($222,600,000). But what are the actual facts, what are the figures for this decade of 1850 to 1860? They are, for the net ordinary expenditures, five hundred and forty-five million five hundred thousand dollars ($545,500,000), and for gross expenditures, six hundred and forty-five million eight hundred thousand dollars ($645,800,000), thus presenting the astonishing and almost incredible excess of expenditure of three hundred and twenty-three million dollars ($323,000,000), or about one hundred million dollars ($100,000,000) more than double the average expenditure in the same length of time by the old Republican party. There is, there can be, but one answer, one explanation to this vast consumption of money in a time of profound peace. It is this : The Democratic leaders and managers must have squandered, plundered, and stolen a large portion of this vast amount during the ten years from 1850 to 1860. And thus were carried out the ten-thousand-times-repeated Democratic promises of economy and reform, and thus were demonstrated the ten-thousand-times-repeated charges of extravagance, robbery, and plunder against the old Republicans, led by John Quincy Adams, and equally false ones against such leaders as Clay, Webster, and Calhoun , and thus, too, was demonstrated the utter absence of truth and patriotism of an organization which has, in all stages of its existence, done all it could to distract, impoverish, and destroy national economy and progress, or to say the least, the utter absence of any power or disposition in a Democratic party to produce any moral, political, or economical reform or improvement, while in pursuit or in possession of supreme power.

It is true, from 1840 to 1860 nearly all materials, goods, and merchandise which enter into the consumption of government, and all kinds of labor and salaries, were largely augmented in price during those twenty years, as they have been vastly more augmented since that time, by the vast productions of gold and silver, and the consequent increase of paper currency. But after making all due allowance for all those things, there stand at least two hundred millions of dollars ($200,000,000) to be accounted for, or rather charged up to the Democratic squander, plunder, and stealage account, from 1850 to 1860. Such extravagance and robbery naturally take place, or rather unavoidably take place, in a party whose chief element of strength is ignorance and depravity, or in any party which has no conscience, no moral sense, and no rule of conduct or strength but " the cohesive power of public plunder."

A RETURN TO FORMER HISTORY.

But having been led into the presentation of these facts and figures by our line of argument, we must now return to the days of Jackson, Benton, and Van Buren.

It is sometimes the case that wise and prudent men deem it best to direct their blows against the apparent rather than the real authors of the evils they are seeking to correct. Hence Clay, Calhoun, and Webster directed their arguments against Jackson and his regular Cabinet rather than his "kitchen cabinet," headed by Benton, and backed by the ignorance and depravity of the country, which this cabinet kept in line by the free use of public plunder. And having now sketched the prominent features of the present Democratic party from its origin up to or near the time when it embarked in its crowning crime by plunging the country into a terrible civil war, I will now close these remarks for the present, and present a passage or two from that grand old patriot and master of oratory, Henry Clay. In a speech delivered in the Senate of the United States, in February, 1838, he says:

" Mr. President, we all have but too melancholy a consciousness of the unhappy condition of our country. We all too well know that our noble and gallant ship lies helpless and immovable upon breakers, dismasted, the surge beating over her venerable sides, and the crew threatened with instantaneous destruction. How came she there? Who was the pilot at the helm when she was stranded? The party in power! The pilot was aided by all the science and skill, by all the charts and instruments, of such distinguished navigators as Washington, the Adamses, Jefferson, Madison, and Monroe, and yet he did not or could not save the public vessel. She was placed in her present miserable condition by his bungling navigation, or by his want of skill and judgment. It is impossible for him to escape from one or the other horn of that dilemma. I leave him at liberty to choose between them."

Speaking of Jackson personally, he said:

" His egotism and vanity prompted him to subject every thing to his will; to change, to remould, and to retouch every thing. Hence the proscription which characterized his administration, the universal expulsion from office, at home and abroad, of all who were not devoted to him, and the attempt to render the Executive department of government, to use a favorite expression of his own, a complete 'unit.' Hence his seizure of the public deposits in the Bank of the United States, and his desire to unite the purse with the sword. Hence his attack upon all the systems of policy which he found in practical operation, on that of internal improvements, and

on that of the protection of national industry.   He
was animated by the same sort of ambition which
induced the master-mind of the age, Napoleon
Bonaparte, to impress his name upon every thing in
France."

And again, he says:

" His administration consisted of astounding
measures, which fell on the public ear like repeated bursts of loud and appalling thunder. Before
the reverberations of one peal had ceased, another
and another came, louder and louder, and more
terrifying.   Or rather, it was like a volcanic mountain, emitting frightful eruptions of burning lava.
Before one was cold and crusted, before the voices of
the inhabitants of buried villages and cities were
hushed in eternal silence, another more desolating
was vomited forth, extending wider and wider the
circle of death and destruction."

Thus was planted in the Democratic party of this
country the seeds, the principles, and practice, and
thus was laid the machinery and the train, which culminated in the greatest of all political crimes—a
cruel civil war in this country among a homogeneous
people, and precisely such a crime and crimes as are
always engendered in a Democratic party when long
in possession of supreme power.

Whether in Greece, in France, in America, or any
other country, the history and fruits of a Democratic
party have always been the same. Ignorance and
depravity, its chief supports, always go hand-in-hand
with dishonesty, corruption, and despotism; and all
these being the chief characteristics of a Democratic

party, its best men are thrust aside, and its most audacious ones become installed as leaders. But no party whose chief element and strength are ignorance and depravity can long rule any people without plunging them into war, anarchy, or despotism : first, because plunder and spoils are not elements of liberty and justice ; and second, because intelligence, virtue, and morality cannot afford to be ruled by ignorance and depravity, and cannot and will not submit to such rule, except temporarily for the sake of peace and harmony, or rather for the sake of exemption from bloodshed, as our fathers did in the days of Benton, Van Buren, and Jackson. If the people of this country ever accept as despot a howling demagogue he will most assuredly be a full-fledged Democrat, surrounded by a host of ignorance and depravity, such as surrounded and upheld Pericles and Alcibiades in Greece, Cæsar and Octavius in Rome ; Marat, Danton, Robespierre, and, finally, Napoleon Bonaparte, in France, with their feet on the necks of the most intelligent and virtuous of the people. We repeat, no other than a Democratic party could ever have brought on the great calamity of a great civil war in this country. Hence the just conclusion is, that but for the Democratic party, the great problem of slavery in this country would probably have been solved, and universal freedom have been ultimately established by peaceable means.

CHAPTER XXVI.

CONCLUSION.

GEN. JACKSON informs us in his last annual message, December, 1836, that there were in the treasury of the United States forty-one million dollars ($41,000,000). Some of this large amount of money went as surplus-revenue distribution among the States, where, in those evil times, it was mainly absorbed or squandered by corrupt politicians. But a large portion of it was lost or stolen by the defaulting deposit banks, and other agents where it had been placed by the Administration for safe-keeping when taken from the Bank of the United States. Had this money, or a part of it, been judiciously applied to internal improvement and other objects counted legitimate by the fathers of the republic, but from which Democratic management had diverted it, it might, to say the least, have greatly mitigated the fearful and destructive crash that came upon the country in less than six months after this message was delivered, and in two months after Jackson's retirement from, and Martin Van Buren's accession to, the Presidency, whereupon the latter called an extra session of Congress to authorize him to borrow money to save the government from utter bankruptcy and ruin until more propitious times.

About this time it was ascertained that out of

some sixty-five Democratic land-agents in the Western States, all except five or six had proved to be defaulters, thus robbing the government of large sums of money. Near the close of his last administration, Gen. Jackson told Mr. Webster he had always sought honest men for the offices, but nearly all turned out to be thieves as soon as they obtained full possession of the places. Three leading and prominent Democrats connected with the Customs of New York—namely, Swartwout, Hoyt, and Price, pocketed more than two million dollars of the collected revenues—Swartwout a million and a half, Hoyt and Price about three hundred thousand dollars each, and made their escape with their booty and families to Europe where they spent the balance of their days, as we may suppose, in " riotous living," and in extolling the greatness of Gen. Jackson, Col. Benton, and the Democratic party of America.

And here, too, we must not neglect to refer to William M. Tweed, of New York City, for several years the leader, or rather "the boss," as he was called, of the Tammany Society and the city Democracy, which has ever been a potent and pivotal force in the national as well as in the city and State politics. It is true, Tweed and his gang of robbers did not hold national offices, yet they were so prominent and influential in connection with Tammany, and exerted so much influence, both in the politics of New York State and the nation, that it would be a material omission in a survey like this to fail to call attention to this piece of Democratic history. In brief, through, and by the means of, the Tammany Society and the management and tactics well known to most Democratic leaders, Tweed was enabled to assume almost imperial powers, and to abstract royal sums from the city treasury. According to the best estimate that could be made, he, with the assistance of his associates, plundered the city, and passed into their own pockets more than thirteen million dollars ($13,000,000), none or very little of which was ever recovered back to the city treasury. Nor was this all. Mr. D. C. McMillan, in a work entitled " The Elective Franchise," endorsed by ex-Gov. Horatio Seymour, remarks: " The Democratic majority of 50,000 in the city would lead Mr. Tweed to give no concern to the election. Established in the primaries, his power was fixed as firmly as a rock." After speaking of the " Canal Ring," which operated in conjunction with Tweed, and robbed the State of New York of many millions, he said: " The tax-payers were bound hand and foot through them, and compelled to meet the expenses of the experiments. The thousand schemes, springing from one centre, inaugurated by the legislative power, increased the debt of the city of New York nearly one hundred million dollars ($100,000,000), and that of the State outside nearly the same amount—all in the space of three years."

As a part of this piece of history, and as a sample of the elements of which our present Democratic party is largely composed, and especially at its head centre in the city of New York, it should be mentioned that before the present election laws were there in force, it was not uncommon for more votes to be counted and returned to head-quarters than there were men, women, and children in the strong Democratic wards from which they came, and that after the Tweed robberies had been exposed by the New York *Times*, he, Tweed, was elected to the State Senate by more than ten thousand majority.

With these historical facts, views, and comments, perhaps in some instances too sharply expressed, may not an old man and an old Whig, who has witnessed the entire course and conduct of our present Democratic party, be allowed herein to propound the following additional questions for the candid consideration of all patriotic readers?

First. Has any Democratic party ever been known to lead in any great moral, political, or economical reform?

Second. Has any Democratic party ever been known to extend the area of freedom or break the shackles of slavery among its own countrymen?

Third. Do we not learn from its history in Greece, its history in France, and its history in the United States, that a Democratic party has an inveterate propensity of casting off its best leaders, and substituting in their places the most audacious and unscrupulous ones it can find in its own or its opponents' ranks?

Fourth. Do not all intelligent men know that the measures and instincts of a Democratic party are not so much against its opponents as against the existence of the government itself?

Fifth. Does not every well-read man know that the leading propensity of a Democratic party is revolution upon revolution until despotism or anarchy is reached? or, what is the same thing, that it can only find a full expression of its nature and instincts in a despotic leader; or, in other words, does not every intelligent man know that each and every Democratic party that ever existed has contained the very elements and forces which have led the way to the overthrow of all free governments which have heretofore existed, thus entitling such a party to be regarded by the world at large as a synonym of anarchy or an ally of despotism?

Sixth. It is true that a Democratic party is the natural and spontaneous outgrowth of free institutions. But is it not also true that this naturalness and instinctiveness come mainly from ignorance and depravity, and from passion and prejudice against stable government, and an ambition to overthrow and trample underfoot the most worthy and patriotic statesmen, and if so, should not such a party be discarded by all honest men?

Seventh. Is it not true that if a Democratic party could be induced to change its name for any other title in the English or any other language, that its morals and habits would be greatly improved, or its danger to free institutions vastly diminished?

Such is the record of Democracy as a Party Name and Organization, which the writer has felt bound to compile and give to the public, hoping it may accomplish some good to our beloved country. He submits the whole, including his comments, to the candid judgment and criticism of all who may read them.

But we must now bring this piece of history to a close, and, in doing so, some readers may ask why this halt is called at or near the time when the great Democratic Rebellion was about to take place? Why not, some may say, go on with the narration of the party's acts and deeds, so full of interest and tragic results, and which filled the world with wonder and astonishment?

In the first place, a complete and comprehensive history was not the chief object of these chapters. Their aim has been to present an historical picture of Democracy as a party name and organization only. Secondly, the time has not come for the true merits or demerits of the characters, acts, and events of the war to be estimated. Alexander H. Stephens, in writing his ponderous volumes on "The War Between the States," as he called it, was so taken up in defending the Democratic party and the State-sovereignty dogma, which, above all other things, was effective in inaugurating the war, that he said but little about the war itself. In the third place, it was not the design of this work to stir up sectional strife, bitterness, or animosity, or fan the smouldering embers of the bloody conflict into life, now happily cooling off and sinking into oblivion, where time, patriotism, and love of peace should, and, we trust, will, soon consign them all. Nor is it intended by these chapters to deny that there are a great many good men in the Democratic party, however misled and mistaken they may be.

But there are some acts and measures of, and some positions taken by, the Democratic party as a whole since "mild-eyed peace smiled upon the land" which are so inconsistent, contradictory, and absurd, and so characteristic of the party, that they can not and should not be passed over in silence,

In the first place, at the close of the war its leaders were clamorous and persistent for an inflation of the currency, which was already, as a consequence of the war, much swollen. If this attempt had succeeded, the result would have been the complete financial ruin of the government and the country. In 1868 it also declared in favor of the taxation of the government bonds and the payment of the same in paper currency. These measures, if adopted, would have consigned the government and country to infamy for the next hundred years. In 1872 the party declared "for a speedy return to specie payments," knowing that such a movement at that time must have been a failure. In 1876 it denounced the law for resumption of specie payments in 1879 up to the very day when resumption took place, all the while demanding its repeal. In 1868 it denounced reconstruction as "revolutionary and void," but in 1876 it declared "its devotion to the amendments of the Constitution" of the United States, thereby contradicting itself and giving its approval to reconstruction.

In 1868 it declared for "such incidental protection to domestic manufactures, as will, without impairing the revenue, best promote and encourage the industrial interests of the country." In 1872 it declared that there was "an irreconcilable difference of opinion with regard to the systems of protection and free trade." In 1876, and in 1880, it declared for a "tariff for revenue only," thus maintaining its consistency for inconsistency and contradiction of its own principles and positions; and thus in this short piece of history, within the memory of everybody, proving the correctness and reliability of the picture of the party the writer has sought to present.

With State sovereignty as its unchangeable and time-honored tenet; with such a record as the history of a Democratic party presents; with its mythological and Janus-faced name to captivate, deceive, and mislead; with an organization whose principles —State sovereignty excepted—are carried about in the hats of its leaders, and tossed up and down, backward and forward, like the balls of an acrobat or the boomerang of a Chinaman; with an organization in which the will and word of its leaders is the law of the rank and file, and as absolute as that of a military commander, ordering them to advance, retreat, or wheel about like soldiers; with the influence of the entire alcoholic and intoxicating beverage interests of the country at its command; with a million grog-shops, gambling-shops, and other dens of iniquity for its recruiting-stations; with ignorance, intemperance, passion, and prejudice as its chief aliment and dependence on the day of election; with no sufficient element or influence within itself to act as a balance-wheel or check upon its wrong-doing; with all, or nearly all, the vagaries, vices, and ambitions which have hitherto undermined and uprooted free institutions and a Republican form of government; with a Pericles, a Mirabeau, a Burr, a Benton, or a Ben Butler as its commander-in-chief, and a Tweed as its typical boss; with a history which shows but too distinctly that the greater and more numerous the crimes it commits, the more wreck and ruin it produces, the stronger it grows, until the horrid war it breeds dashes it to pieces, who can say that such a party should have the confidence and support of a great nation with well-established Republican institutions and convictions?

What fearful strides, what fearful movements, backward or forward, reactionary or direct, may not such a party adopt? and what tricks may it not play " before high Heaven," outstripping in despotism and oppression the capacity of kings and emperors to inflict? and what havoc may it not make, as it has often made, with all that is sacred, venerable, and valuable in morals, in politics, and even in civilization itself, if again in possession of supreme power? Although many of its members are virtuous and patriotic, it is not in the nature of things, nor in the nature of intellect, nor in accordance with the laws of God, for such a party to govern a great people wisely or successfully, or to allow peace, prosperity, and good-fellowship to remain in the land. What authority or influence, moral, political, or religious, can restrain such a party, when, with no fixed principles, and a time-honored practice of casting off its best men and seeking for leaders the most audacious and unscrupulous in its own or its opponents' ranks, it casts its greedy eyes upon, and sees within its reach, the millions and hundreds of millions in the treasury of a great nation, and the vast amounts of wealth which industry, enterprise, and skill have developed under a mild and wise administration of the government and laws?

The history of such a party in Greece, the history of such a party in France, with its terrible record, the history of such a party in this country from 1829 to 1861, while in possession of supreme power, as well as its shuffling methods and principles since the close of the war, all present the same kind of results, and should warn the American people in unmistakable tones to restrain this party now and forever from the control of our government and its Republican institutions.

And, finally, inasmuch as we all know that the Democracy is a large and well-organized party; inasmuch as we all believe it contains many good men who wish well to the government and the nation; but inasmuch as we all know, and all its leaders and organs know, that its history is stained through and through with all the crimes and all the calamities that are possible to attach to, or spring from, any party; inasmuch as we all know, and all its leaders know, that its measures, so far as they have pertained to the internal affairs of the country, have been radically and irredeemably wrong: therefore, all these things combined ought to consign the party to condemnation and oblivion forever.

If the old Federal party, with Washington, Hamilton, and John Adams as its chiefs, after constructing and putting into operation the Constitution of the United States, and after twelve years of faithful service without a stain upon its escutcheon, had to retire from the political arena; if the old Republican party, with Jefferson and Madison as its chiefs, after twenty-five years of honorable service, had to give place to a ranting and raving Democratic party; if the Whig party of 1832, after twenty years of faithful warfare for the right against the wrong, with J. Q. Adams, Clay, and Webster as its chiefs, had to retire from the field, why should not this same Democratic party, after more than fifty years of blunders, wrongs, and crimes of the deepest dye against its country, with hardly a redeeming trait or quality to commend it, be consigned to eternal oblivion by the people of the United States? and echo answers why not? for if any one of the blunders, wrongs, and crimes of the Democratic party had been committed by any other party, it would remand it to the minority at once. Why not then consign this Democratic party to the minority forever? Disguise the matter as its leaders may, the Democratic party of to-day still contains all the elements, essence, and animus adapted to the overthrow of Republican institutions and well-regulated liberty upon the American continent, and unquestionably presents to the American people, as it has done for the past fifty years, the alternative to overthrow and consign it to oblivion, or to have their institutions eventually overthrown and destroyed by this party. Again, suffer it to acquire supreme power, it will thresh the land with flails of iron or the harrow of anarchy, until its inhabitants, like the Israelites of old, cry out in their agony for a king, or again seek relief in a dismemberment of this great and glorious Union.

The writer has now performed, according to his best ability, the task indicated in the introductory chapter of this work, and if, in doing so, he has fallen into the style of partisan controversy, he asks to have the responsibility for the fault, if fault it be, ascribed to the characteristics of the era in which we live. Burke and Chatham dealt largely in invective, and Junius poured out a flood of denunciation against parties, lords, and monarchs; and from such denunciations some of our most valuable political lessons have been derived, and by the use of them many political evils have been eradicated. Why, then, may not political teachers of to-day, in fighting their battles in behalf of good government, be guided by such illustrious examples? If, in performing this labor, the writer has sought to expose only the vices and dangers of one of the great parties of our country, and has therefore laid himself open to the charge of being one-sided, it should be remembered that the opponents of the other great party have the same privilege, and that it is mainly by sustained discussion between opponents that sound and just principles can be secured in all departments of society. No one has been able to produce axioms and arguments for all parties to any controversy. Should other writers of the day deem it patriotic to present a history of the Republican party, or of any other party of our country, the people should be ready to give due consideration to their conclusions and criticisms. As stated in the opening chapter, the writer has contented himself with exposing and commenting upon Democracy as a Party Name and Political Organization. The defence of the party against this arraignment, and the exposure of the blunders and crimes of its opponents, present work for others.

THE END.

www.ingramcontent.com/pod-product-compliance
Lightning Source LLC
Chambersburg PA
CBHW030316270326
41926CB00010B/1394

*9 7 8 3 3 3 7 0 7 8 8 1 2 *